Glossary of Arabic terms

(An Islamic dictionary)

SAUL SILAS FATHI

Ingram / Lightningsource.com

Glossary of Arabic terms: An Islamic dictionary

Copyright 2012 by Saul Silas Fathi

Library of Congress Number: 2012918529

ISBN#: 978-0-9777117-4-1   Trade paper

Book Design: Fran Padro

Cover design: Anthony Spano

This book was printed in the United States of America

Other books by Saul Silas Fathi:

1. Full Circle: Escape from Baghdad and the return
    ISBN# 978-0-9777117-8-9 (Trade paper)
2. History of the Jews and Israel
    ISBN# 978-0-9777117-3-4 (Trade paper)
3. Islamic leaders: Their biographies and
    accomplishments
    (From Muhammad to the present)
    ISBN# 978-0-9777117-5-8 (Trade paper)

Saul Silas Fathi

ACKNOWLEDGEMENT

I owe deep gratitude to Elaine Lanmon and

Fran Padro for their assistance in typing,

editing and researching this manuscript; for their

patience, their valuable advice and dedication

to this massive project.

***

3

Author/Lecturer: Saul Silas Fathi

Saul Silas Fathi was born to a prominent Jewish family in Baghdad, Iraq. At age 10, he was smuggled out of Baghdad through Iran and eventually reached the state of Israel. He began writing a diary at age 11 and had several stories published in Israeli youth magazines. In 1958, he worked his way to Brazil where he nearly starved. In 1960, he came to the U.S. on a student exchange visa. After Basic Training in Fort Benning, Georgia, he was sent to helicopter school at Fort Bragg, North Carolina, and there enrolled at the University of Virginia. Within a few months, Saul was shipped to South Korea where he served with the 1st Cavalry Division, 15th Aviation Company, the famed helicopter division in the Vietnam War. Saul retired in 2003 and began writing his memoirs, Full Circle: Escape from Baghdad and the return. Today, he lives in Long Island, New York, with his wife Rachelle. He is also a certified linguist, fluent in English, Hebrew, Arabic, and Portuguese.

Mr. Fathi has lectured at 160+ organizations since 2006, and authored 3 books: "Full Circle: Escape from Baghdad and the return" (ISBN#978-0-977117-8-9) and "History of the Jews and Israel"(ISBN# 978-0-9777117-3-4). And "Islamic Leaders" (ISBN# 978-0-9777117-5-8)

Mr. Fathi will be publishing a new book: "Glossary of Arabic terms (an Islamic dictionary)"

www.saulsilasfathi.com / fathi@optonline.net

***

T.O.C. Glossary of Arabic terms

Introduction:
Glossary of Arabic terms: An Islamic dictionary

Dear reader: In this book you will be introduced to hundreds of Arabic terms, an extensive Islamic Dictionary. They are presented in alphabetical order.

History of Islam:

In less than a century after Muhammad's death Islam swept through Asia, Africa and Europe, dominating an area larger than that of the Roman Empire at its peak. Today, one in 5 people on the face of this earth is a Muslim. A total of 1.6 billion people; the second largest religion in the world and the fastest-growing.

For a period of 400 years, from the Eighth to the Twelfth Century, the achievements of this synthesized culture were unsurpassed. In fact, much of the science and literature of the European Renaissance was inspired by Islamic models. I Urge everyone to learn about it.

Islam (=Submission): Is the monotheistic religion articulated by the Qur'an, a text considered by its adherents to be the verbatim word of God (Arabic: *Allāh*), and by the teachings and normative example (called the *Sunnah* and composed of *Hadith*) of Muhammad, considered by them to be the last prophet of God. An adherent of Islam is called a *Muslim*.

God (Allah): Muslims believe that God is one and incomparable and the purpose of existence is to worship God. Muslims also believe that Islam is the complete and universal version of a primordial faith that was revealed at many times and places before,

7

including through Abraham, Moses and Jesus, whom they consider prophets. They maintain that previous messages and revelations have been partially changed or corrupted over time, but consider the Qur'an to be both the unaltered and the final revelation of God.

Islam's most fundamental concept is a rigorous monotheism, called Tawhid. God is described in chapter 112 of the Qur'an as: "Say: He is God, the One and Only; God, the Eternal, Absolute; He begetteth not, not is He begotten; and there is none like unto Him." **(Qur'an 112:1-4)** Muslims repudiate the Christian doctrine of the Trinity and divinity of Jesus, comparing it to polytheism, but accept Jesus as a prophet. In Islam, God is beyond all comprehension and Muslims are not expected to visualize God.

Muslims believe that creation of everything in the universe is brought into by God's sheer command "'Be' and so it is." and that the purpose of existence is to worship God. He is viewed as a personal God who responds whenever a person in need or distress calls Him. There are no intermediaries, such as clergy, to contact God who states "We are nearer to him than (his) jugular vein" *Allāh* is the term with no plural or gender used by Muslims and Arabic-speaking Christians and Jews meaning the one God.

Holy Qur'an: It is divided into 114 suras, or chapters, which combined contain 6,236 *āyāt*, or verses. Muslim jurists consult the H*adith*, or the written record of Prophet Muhammad's life, to both supplement the Qur'an and assist with its interpretation. The science of Qur'anic commentary and exegesis is known as T*afsir*. To Muslims, the Qur'an is perfect only as revealed in the original Arabic; translations are necessarily deficient because of language difference, the fallibility of translators, and the impossibility of preserving the original's inspired style.

Predestination: In accordance with the Islamic belief in predestination, or divine preordainment (*al-qadā wa'l-qadar*), God has full knowledge and control over all that occurs. For Muslims, everything in the world that occurs, good or evil, has been preordained and nothing can happen unless permitted by God. According to Muslim theologians, although events are preordained, man possesses FREE WILL in that he has the faculty to choose between right and wrong, and is thus responsible for his actions.

Five Pillars of Islam

The Pillars of Islam (*Arkan al-Islam*; also *Arkan ad-din*, "pillars of religion") are five basic acts in Islam, considered obligatory of all believers. The Quran presents them as a framework for worship and a sign of commitment to the faith. They are (1) Shahadah (Creed), (2) daily prayers (Salat), (3) Almsgiving (Zakah), (4) Fasting during Ramadan (Sawm), and (5) Pilgrimage to Mecca (Hajj) at least once in a lifetime. The Shi'a and Sunni sects both agree on the essential details for the performance of these acts.

1. **Testimony** (*Shahadah*)
   The Shahadah, which is the basic creed of Islam that must be recited under oath with the specific statement: " *'ashadu 'al-lā ilah illā-llāhu wa 'ashadu 'anna Muhammadan rasūlu-llāh*", or "I testify there are no deities other than God alone and I testify that Muhammad is the Messenger of God." Muslims must repeat the S*hahadah* in prayer, and non-Muslims wishing to convert to Islam are required to recite the creed.

2. **Prayer** (*Salah*)
   Ritual prayers, calledS alāh or S alāt, must be performed five times a day. Salah is intended to focus the mind on God, and is seen as a personal communication with Him that expresses

gratitude and worship. Salah is compulsory but flexibility in the specifics is allowed depending on circumstances. The prayers are recited in the Arabic language, and consist of verses from the Qur'an.

- **Mosque (Masjid)**
  A mosque is in place of worship is a place of worship for Muslims, who often refer to it by its Arabic name, *Masjid*. The word *Mosque* in English refers to all types of buildings dedicated to Islamic worship.   Although the primary purpose of the mosque is to serve as a place of prayer, it is also important to the Muslim community as a place to meet and study.   Shi'a Islam permits combining prayers in succession.

3. **Fasting** (*Sawm of Ramadan*)
Fasting, from food, drink and sex must be performed from dawn to dusk during the month of Ramadhan. The fast is to encourage a feeling of nearness to God, and during it Muslims should express their gratitude for and dependence on Him, atone for their past sins, and think of the needy.   But missed fasts usually must be made up quickly.   The fasting ends daily at sun-down and continues for 30 days.

4. **Alms-giving** (*Zakat and Sadaqah*)
"Zakat" is giving a fixed portion of accumulated wealth by those who can afford it to help the poor or needy, and also to assist the spread of Islam. It is considered a religious obligation (as opposed to voluntary charity) that the well-off owe to the needy because their wealth is seen as a "trust from God's bounty". The Qur'an and the Hadith also suggest a Muslim give even more as an act of voluntary alms-giving (*Sadaqah*).

5. **Pilgrimage** (*Hajj*)
The pilgrimage, called the H*ajj* during the Islamic month of *Dhu al-Hijjah* in the city of Mecca. Every able-bodied Muslim who can afford it must make the pilgrimage to Mecca at least once in his or her lifetime. Rituals of the Hajj include walking seven times around the Kaaba, touching the black stone if possible, walking or running seven times between Mount Safa and Mount Marwah, and symbolically stoning the Devil in Mina.

Jihad and the Military: Jihad means "to strive or struggle" (in the way of God) and is considered the "Sixth Pillar of Islam" by a minority of Sunni Muslim authorities. Jihad, in its broadest sense, is classically defined as "exerting one's utmost power, efforts, endeavors, or ability in contending with an object of disapprobation. Jihad, when used without any qualifier, is understood in its military aspect. Jihad also refers to one's striving to attain religious and moral perfection. Some Muslim authorities, especially among the Shi'a and Sufis, distinguish between the "greater jihad", which pertains to spiritual self-perfection, and the "lesser jihad", defined as warfare.

Within Islamic jurisprudence, jihad is usually taken to mean military exertion against non-Muslim combatants in the defense or expansion of the Ummah. Others have argued that the goal of Jihad is global conquest. Jihad is the only form of warfare permissible in Islamic law and may be declared against terrorists, criminal groups, rebels, apostates, and leaders or states that oppress Muslims or hamper proselytizing efforts.

Under most circumstances and for most Muslims, jihad is a collective duty (*Fard Kifaya*): Its performance by some individuals exempts the others. For most Shi'as, offensive jihad can only be declared by a divinely appointed leader of the Muslim community, and as such is suspended since Muhammad al-Mahdi's occultation in 868 AD.

Muhammad (610-632): Muhammad (570–June 8, 632) was a trader later becoming a religious, political, and military leader. However, Muslims do not view Muhammad as the creator of Islam, but instead regard him as the last messenger of God, through which the Qur'an was revealed. Muslims view Muhammad as the restorer of the original, uncorrupted monotheistic faith of Adam, Abraham, Moses, Jesus, and other prophets.

For the last 22 years of his life, beginning at age 40 in 610 CE, Muhammad started receiving revelations that he believed to be from God. The content of these revelations, known as the Qur'an, was memorized and recorded by his companions. During this time, Muhammad preached to the people of Mecca, imploring them to abandon polytheism. After 12 years of preaching, Muhammad and the Muslims performed the Hijah ("emigration") to the city of Medina (formerly known as *Yathrib*) and the Meccan migrants (*Muhajirun*), Muhammad established his political and religious authority. By 630 Muhammad was victorious in the nearly bloodless Conquest of Mecca, and by the time of his death in 632 (at the age of 63) he untied the tribes of Arabia into a single religious polity.

Rise of the caliphate and civil war (632–750):
With Muhammad's death in 632, disagreement broke out over who would succeed him as leader of the Muslim community. Umar ibn

al-Khattab, a prominent companion of Muhammad, nominated Abu Bakr, who was Muhammad's companion and close friend. Others added their support and Abu Bakr was made the First Caliph.

- **The Rashidun (Rightly-Guided Caliphs):**
  Abu Bakr's death in 634 resulted in the succession of Umar ibn al-Khattab as the caliph, followed by Uthman ibn al-Affan, Ali ibn Abi Talib and Hasan ibn Ali. The first 4 caliphs are known as *al-khulafa' ar-rāshidūn* ("Rightly Guided Caliphs"). Under them, the territory under Muslim rule expanded deeply into Persian and Byzantine territories. When Umar was assassinated in 644, the election of Uthman as successor was met with increasing opposition. In 656, Uthman was also killed, and Ali assumed the position of caliph. After fighting off opposition in the first civil war (the "First Fitna"), Ali was assassinated by Kharijites in 661. Following this, Mu'awiyah seized power and began the Umayyad dynasty, with its capital in Damascus.

Islamic Accomplishments:
Islamic civilization flourished in what is sometimes referred to as the "Islamic Golden Age". Public hospitals established during this time, are considered "the first hospitals" in the modern sense of the word, and issued the first medical diplomas to license doctors of medicine. The Guinness World Records recognizes the University of Al Karaouine, founded in 859, as the world's older degree-granting university. An important pioneer in this, Ibn al-Haytham is regarded as the father of the modern scientific method and often referred to as the "world's first true scientist." Discoveries include gathering the data used by Copernicus for his heliocentric conclusions

13

and Al-Jahiz's proposal of the theory of natural selection. Rumi wrote some of the finest Persian poetry and is still one of the best selling poets in America. Legal institutions introduced include the trust and charitable trust (Waqf).

***

GLOSSARY OF ARABIC TERMS:
(AN ISLAMIC DICTIONARY)

The following list consists of notable concepts that are derived from both Islamic and Arab tradition, which are expressed as words in the Arabic language. One of the complexities of the Arabic language is that a single word can have multiple meanings. The word *Islam* is itself a good example.

A.H.: Abbr. of After Hijra. The Islamic era began with the migration of the Prophet Muhammad from Mecca to Medina on A.D. 15 July 622

Aabru: Dignity

Al Saud: see House of Saud

Aal: Of a family or tribe

Abaya: A black over garment, either a large square or fabric draped from the shoulders or head or long caftan. It is the traditional form of Islamic dress for women in many countries of the Arabian Peninsula, and it is sometimes adopted in other parts of the Islamic world. The Abaya covers the whole body except the face, feet and hands. It can be worn with the niqab, a face veil covering all but the eyes. Some women also wear black gloves to cover their hands. Islamic outer garment; worn outside house.

Abd: Servant, worshipper, slave. Muslims consider themselves servants and slaves of God. Common Muslim names such

15

as Abdullah (servant of God), Abdul Malik (Slave of the King), Abdur Rahman (Slave of the most Beneficent), Abdus Salam (Slave of peace), all refer to names of Allah. Servant or slave; as in 'Abdallah, servant of God.

Abdallah: Servant of God, acknowledging God as Creator, Guide and Judge. .

Ablution: Required washing of the arms, face, head and feet prior to praying, reading the Koran, or engaging in other acts of worship.

Abu: A father in Arab society is traditionally referred to by the name of his first born son.

Achoura: Celebration of the tenth day of the Hegira month of Moharram, when Shiites commemorate the martyrdom of Imam Hussein at Karbala on October 10, 680.

Adab: A genre of prose literature developed in Damascus by the Umayyads. The most famous was the Genial Al-Jahiz (d. 868). New literature developed during the Abbasid caliphate.

Adab: Muslim manners, proper behavior (Arabia/South Asia); also called **riwaj** or custom in Afghanistan and Pakistan.

Adam: The first man, created by Allah out of clay. Known as the father of humankind and the first prophet.

Adha: Sacrifice [Arabic]

Adhan: Call to prayer given five times daily; *Mu'adhdhin* – the one to give the call. Sometimes alternatively spelled and pronounced Azaan and Adhan.

16

adil/adila: Just

Adl: Equilibrium, balance (important Qur'anic concept). Justice especially distributive justice, social, economic, political and environmental.

Ahad: Literally "one". Islamically ahad means One Alone, unique, none like God. Al Wahid is one of the names of God.

Ahadith (singular, hadith): News, reports. Documented traditions of the teachings and actions of the Prophet Muhammad, which were not in the Quran but which were recorded for posterity by his close companions and the members of his family.

Aham: The heart. Muhammad can be defined as the beauty of the heart [**aham**] reflected in the face [**muham**].

ahd (dar al): Land of contractual peace in Islamic doctrine; zone where Muslims can live in peace in a non-Muslim state. (Covenant): in 2: 27, for instance, refers to the command issued by God to His servants. This ahd consists of God's eternal command that His creatures are obligated to render their service, obedience and worship to Him alone.

Ahkam: Rulings and orders of the Quran and Sunnah. Five kinds of orders: Wajib, Mustahab, Muharram, Makruh and Halal.

Ahl al Bayt: "People of the house of Muhammad" Members of Muhammad's household. Also known among Shia as the Ma'sumin (in fallible, spiritually pure)

Ahl al Fatrah: People who live in ignorance of the teachings of a revealed religion, but according to the Fitra,the natural

17

religion innate to human nature as created by God.

Ahl al-Bayt: "People of the House," referring to the members of the Prophet's family; descendants of the Prophet's son-in-law 'Ali. The household of the Prophet; those Muslims loyal to the Prophet's immediate family, specifically 'Ali, his wife, Fatimah, and their two sons, Hasan and Husayn; Shi'ites, defining themselves apart from, and over against, dominant Sunni Muslims.

Ahl al-Dhimmah (or **Dhimmis**): Are the non-Muslim subjects of an Islamic state who have been guaranteed protection of their rights – life, property and practice of their religion, etc. – by the Muslims. are the non Muslim subjects of an Islamic state who have been guaranteed protection of their rights, life property and practice of their religion.

Ahl al-Hadith: Refers to the group of scholars in Islam who pay relatively greater importance to 'traditions' than to other sources of Islamic doctrine such as **qiyas**, and tend to interpret the traditions more literally and rigorously. The term has also come to be used lately for a group of Muslims in the Indo-Pakistan subcontinent who are close to the Hanbali school in theology, and claim to follow no single school on legal matters. Hadith People. A school of thought which first appeared during the Umayyad period, which would not permit jurists to use **ijtihad (q.v.)** but insisted that all legislation is based upon valid **ahadith (q.v.)**

Ahl al-Kitab: People of the Book. The Qur'anic term for people, such as Jews or Christians, who adhered to the earlier scriptures. Since the Prophet and most of the early Muslims were illiterate, and had very few – if any – books, it has been suggested that this term should more accurately be translated: "followers of an earlier revelation." Those who acknowledge God as creator, guide and judge of humankind; Jews, Christians, and others who have a Book that was revealed by God before the final Book, the Qur'an. Also refers to the followers of divine revelation before the advent of the Prophet Muhammad

Ahl I Haqq (Ahl- I Haqq): A branch of Shiite Islam with strong esoteric leanings and centered in Kurdistan

Ahl: People of . . .

Ahlaf: The Confederates

Ahlil Bayt: People of the house

Ahmad **(A):** The state of the heart, the *qalb*, or *aham*. *Ahmad* is the heart of Muhammad. The beauty of the heart [*aham*] is the beauty of the countenance [*muham,* Tamil] of Muhammad. That is the beauty of Allah's qualities. This is a name that comes from within the ocean of divine knowledge [*hahr al-'ilm*]. Allah is the One who is worthy of the praise of the *qalb*, the heart. Lit.: most praiseworthy

Ahman Bin Taymiyya: Jurist...

Ahram: Pyramids

Ajr: Recompense.

Akbar: Greater, one of God's traits, as in Allahu Akbar

Akhbar: Report, news

Akhirah: Hereafter or eternal life … the life of the Hereafter, as opposed to the life of this world (the next life).

Akhlaq: Character traits; virtues, praiseworthy moral and ethical qualities; the science of ethics; the practice of virtue, Morals, see khuluq

Al Akhirah: (After life, Hereafter, Next World). The term embraces the following ideas: 1) That man is answerable to God 2) That the present order of existence will someday come to an end. 3) That when that happens, God will bring another order into being in which He will resurrect all human beings, gather them together and examine their conduct, and reward them with justice and mercy. 4) That those who are reckoned good will be sent to Paradise whereas the evil doers will be consigned to Hell. 5) That the real measure of success or failure of a person is not the extent of his prosperity in the present life, but his success in the Next.

'Alamin: Literally "worlds", humankind, jinn, angels and all that exists

Al Amr Bi'l Maruf: Islamic doctrine of enjoining righteousness

Al An am: Literally 'the cattle', the title of Surah 6 of the Quran

Al Aqsa Intifada: see Second Intifada

Al Asharatu Mubashsharun bil Jannah: Or just Asharatu Mubashsharah (Arabic mubashshirune bil Jannah): the ten companions of Muhammad who were promised paradise only in Sunni Islam

Al Baqara: The longest chapter in the Qur'an

Al Barzakh: The realm in which the souls of the dead live. Literally the "partition"; that is, the time between death and the resurrection.

Al Bayt Al-Muqaddas: A name given to the temple at Jerusalem, on which site the Dome of the Rock stands today. Lit.: the Holy House.

Al Birr: Piety and righteousness and every act of obedience to Allah

Al Faraj: The return of the Shia Mahdi

Al Ferdose: A graveyard for all the martyrs of Iran in war with Iraq

Al Hagag: A kingdom

Al Hamdu Lillah: "Praise be to God" Qur'anic exclamation and also same meaning as hallelujah

Al Ikhlas: Purity of faith. Sincerity. Genuine in religious beliefs.

Al Kaka: A kingdom

Al Khaliq: The Creator, Allah

Al Mahdi: A caliph who is prophesied to appear in the future and lead gruesome battles near the end of time.

Al Massih Al Dajjal: An evil creature that will appear in the time of Al Mahdi and claim he is God. He is one of the major signs of the Last Day.

Al Quds: (*Arabic: the holy—short form of* Beit al Muquodus, *The*

House of Holiness); see Jerusalem

al Sawa al Islamia: The Islamic Awakening, the term sometimes used to refer to the political Islam phenomenon

Al Uzza: One of the goddesses worshipped by the pagan Quraysh

Al: The Arabic definite article al is frequently used with proper nouns, especially places and people. For instance, Basra is written as al Basra in Arabia and Nur al Din Attasi as Nur al din al Attasi.

Al-A'rab Signifies the Bedouin – whether of the desert of the countryside – in the vicinity of Madina. For a long time they had followed a policy of opportunism with regard to the conflict between Islam and unbelief. However, as Islam established its sway over the greater part of Hijaz and Najd and the power of the tribes hostile to Islam began to weaken, they saw their interests lay in entering the fold of Islam. For details see **Surah** 9, nn. 90 and 95.

Al-akhirah **(A):** The hereafter; the next world; the kingdom of God

Alam **(A)(pl.** *'alamun or alamin***):** The universe; the cosmos; the metaphysical world

Alam al-Arwah: The world of pure souls, where all souls are performing **tasbih**, or prayers of praise to God. ... the world of the spirits, contrasted with the world of the bodies; often called malakut

Alam al-Mithal: The world of pure images. A realm of the human psyche which is the source of the visionary experience of

Muslim mystics and the seat of the creative imagination.

Al-Amin: "The Trustworthy"; a nickname for Muhammad; a reputation he cultivated as a caravan protector.

Alamin: Literally world's humankind, jinn, angels and all that exists

Alamiya: International, world

Al Amr Bi'l Maruf: Islamic doctrine of enjoining right. There exists in Islam the (obligatory) principle of encouraging other people to do the right thing.

Al-Anfal: Literally, 'the spoils of war', and the title of the eighth *sura* of the Qur'an; the codename given by the Iraqi authorities to their forces' operations in Kurdistan in 1988.

Al-Aqsa: see Haram al-Sharif.

Al-Asma Wa'l Sifat: The 99 names and attributes of God (in Islam)

Al-Asma' al-Husna, Literally meaning the 'most excellent names' used of God, express His greatness and paramountcy, holiness, purity, and the perfection and absoluteness of all His attributes.

Al-awwal **(A):** The creation of all forms; the stage at which the soul became surrounded by form and each creation took shape; the stage at which the souls of the six kinds of lives (earth-life, fire-life, water-life, air-life, ether-life, and light-life) were placed in their respective forms. Allah created these forms and then placed that 'trust property' which is life within those forms

Glossary of Arabic Terms

***Alayhi salaatu was salaam*:** Arabic for "upon him be prayers and peace"; an honorific phrase said after Muslims speak the name of a prophet

Alayhis Salam: "Peace be upon him". This expression normally follows after naming a prophet (other than Muhammad), or one of the noble Angels (i.e. Jibreel [Gabriel], Mikaeel [Michael], etc.)

Al-Bari: The Evolver

Al-Batin: Inward, in Sufism

***Al-Bayt al-Muqaddas*:** A name given to the temple at Jerusalem, on which site the Dome of the Rock stands today. Lit.: the Holy House

AL-Dhakil: The Immigrant

Alem: (plural, **ulema** (Arabic) Muslim cleric.

Al-Faruq: The Differentiator (between right and wrong: Umar).

***Al-hamadu lillah* (A):** "All praise is to You." Allah is the glory and greatness that deserves all praise. "You are the One responsible for the appearance of all creations. Whatever appears, whatever disappears, whatever receives benefit or loss – all is Yours. I have surrendered everything into Your hands. I remain with hands out-stretched, spread out, empty, and helpless. Whatever is happening and whatever is going to happen is all Yours." Lit.: All praise belongs to Allah!

Alhumdulillah: God be praised (thank God)

Alif (A): The first letter of the Arabic alphabet (I). To the transformed man of wisdom, the *alif* represents Allah, the One. See also: *lam, mim*

Alim (A) (pl. *'Ulama*): Teacher; learned one, one of wisdom. One who swims in Allah's *ahat* [essence of grace] and has learned the ocean of divine knowledge [*hahr al-'ilm*]. ... one who knows. A scholar, a scientist or a theologian. traditional Islamic scholar.

Alimun Sam'un: Al-Llah is knowing and hearing

Al-Insan Al-Kamil: Muhammad, the most "accomplished" or "perfect" man.

Aliws: The natural successor to the caliphate by reason of his close kinship to the prophet.

Al-Jahiliyyah: The "time of ignorance" or period of Arab paganism preceding the revelation of Islam.

Al-Khaliq: The Creator

Allah Akbar (A): God is Great! "Allah is Most Great." God is Greater (there is none greater than He).

Allah Ta'ala: (A) God Almighty; God is the Highest. **Allah:** (A) the beautiful undiminishing One. Ta'ala (A) the One who exists in all lives in a state of humility and exaltedness.

Allah: God; the first and foremost of the ninety nine Divine Names; the God of Islam. "the {one and unique} god" (**Al-Ilah**); the Creator and Judge of humankind; "The God before Whom there are no others."

Allahu Akbar: God is great (greater).

Allahumma: "O God."

Al-Mahdi: The guided one; caliph

Al-Maqaddimah: Introduction to history by Ibn Khaldun

Al-Mawla: The lord; master.

Alms: Money, food, or other goods given as charity to the poor.

Al-Mu'minum: The believers

Al-Mushrikun: Idolaters, polytheists, disbelievers in the oneness of Allah; pagans.

Al-Mutawattah: The Beaten Path; compiled by Malik ibn Anas

Al-Nakba: Calamity, disaster; term used by Muslims to denote the date of the proclamation of the State of Israel, 15 May 1948.

Al-Ommiyya: The illiterate (Muhammad)

Al-Qa'ida: With definite article, literally, a base; title of the terrorist organization led by Osama bin Laden.

Al-Rabba: The sovereign

Al-Rahib: The monk

Al-Rahim: One of the beautiful ninety-nine names of God – the Most Compassionate. He is the One who redeems, the One who protects from evil, who preserves and who confers eternal bliss; the Savior. On the Day of Judgment and on the Day of Inquiry and on all days from the day of the beginning, He protects and brings His creations back unto Himself.

Al-Rahman: One of the beautiful ninety-nine names of God – the Most Merciful. He is the **Rahman.** He is the King. He is the Nourisher, the One who gives food. He is the Compassionate One. He is the One who protects the creations. He is the Beneficent One.

Al-Rashidun: The rightly-guided caliphs (the first four caliphs: Abu Bakr, Omar, Uthman and Ali).

Al-Sadiq: The Truthful

Al-salam 'alaykum **(A):** "May the peace and peacefulness of Allah be upon you." This is the greeting of love. *Al-salam 'alaykum al-salam.* One heart embraces the other with love and greets it with respect and honor. Both hearts are one. In reply *wa 'alaykum al-salam* means, "May the peace and peacefulness of Allah be upon you also."

Al-Salam 'Alaykum Wa-Rahmat Allah Wa-Barakatuhu Kulluh: (A) May all the peace, the beneficence, and the blessings of God be upon you!

Al-Sawa al-Islamia: The "Islamic Awakening"; the term sometimes used to refer to the political Islam phenomenon.

Al-shahadah kalimah: The second *kalimah*, the witnessing. *Ashhadu an la ilah illa Allah wahdahu la sharik lahu; wa-ashhadu anna Muhammad 'abduhu wa-rasuluh* – I witness (testify) that there is no god other than Allah; He is One without partner, and I witness (testify) that Muhammad is His slave and His Messenger. See also: *kalimah,* appendix

Al-Tahrim: Prohibition

Al-Takhalluq bi Akhlaq Allah: The attributes of God.

Al-Tawhid: The unity of God

Al-Zahir: Outward, in Sufism

Al-Zalzalah: Earthquake

Amaa: General, public

Amal: Cultural practices, hope.

Amanah: The trust, of all creation, only human beings carries the trust which is free will.

Amin: amen supplication meaning "O God accept our invocation!"

Aminah: Muhammad's mother. Aminah fell sick and died in Abwa, near Madina (then Yathrib) when Muhammad was six years old.

Aminyat: security

Amir al-Muminim: Commander of the Faithful; title of certain rulers. Umar Commander of the Believers.

Amir: (and commonly emir): Prince. Originally military, a common title; the ruler in Kuwait. ... lord, endowed with power in the classical Muslim world; chief of a political or military group, especially of an Islamist group. Also written emir, an Arabia title widely used in the Arab lands and beyond as a title of sovereignty and also at some times and in some places as a claim to something less than fully sovereign authority. Amir al Muhammad 'minin, usually translated "Commander of the Faithful," was one of the earliest titles of the caliph its use remained a caliphal prerogative and was interpreted as a claim to supreme Muslim political sovereignty. In Medieval times amir was used more widely by a number of regional rulers exercising effective independence under the nominal suzerainty of the caliph. In modern Saudi Arabia, it has been given to governors of provinces, some important heads of tribes, and some other dignitaries. It was used as a regal title by the ruler of Transjordan until 1946 when it was replaced by king. It is still used in some other Arab principalities known as emirates. At the present day, it is most commonly used to designate members of reigning families other than the sovereign. In this sense, it is customarily translated prince.

Amn: Security

Amr: Command

Amu: Uncle

An Nasikh: Revelation

An'um Muhammad (A): The food; the *rizq*; the nourishment of all creations; Muhammad of the kindness or blessings

Anbiya: Prophets.

Anfal: Property of the Imam

Angel Azrael: The Angel of Death, who captures the souls of the deceased.

Angel Gabriel: The angel who brought down revelations to Allah's messengers, and the one holding the highest position among the angels.

Angel: A creature of light made to obediently serve Allah.

Angra Mainyu: Zoroastrian deity, evil.

Anhrya: (sing. *nabi*) Prophets

Ani, papyrus of: Shows judgment scene from Book of the Dead.

animism: The belief that all natural phenomena have souls and can influence human events.

An-Nisa'i: Imam, a Muslim scholar

Ansar: Means 'the Helpers'. In Islamic parlance the word refers to the Muslims of Madina who helped the **Muhajirun** of Makka in the process of the latter's settling down in the new environment. The Medinese Muslims who became the "helpers" of the Prophet by giving the first Muslims a home when they were forced to leave Mecca in 622, and assisted them in the project of establishing the first Muslim community.

Ansariyas: see Alawis

Anum Muhammad: The food; the **rizq**; the nourishment of all creations; Muhammad of the kindness or blessings.

Aqidah: The Islamic creed, or the six article of faith, which

30

consists of the belief in God, Angels, Messengers and Prophets, scriptures, the Day of Judgment and Destiny.

Aqiqah: The celebration marking the birth of a new baby. Islamic practice of shaving the head of the new born make and contributing the weight in silver for charity as well as 2 lambs. A celebration of slaughter of an animal; first weeks of a child's birth.

Aql: Intelligence, intellect, reason; macrocosmically, the first creation of God, and microcosmically the divine light of guidance innate in every soul

Arabic language: Arabic belongs to the Semitic language family, its sisters being Hebrew and Aramaic and is written from right to left. It has been a written language at least since the early fourth century AD. But the spoken language carries from region to region and there are five major groups of dialects: those found in Iraq, the Arabian Peninsula, Syria, Egypt and North Africa. It is the language of the Koran.

Arafat: A mountain near Mecca.

Arak: An alcoholic drink variously made from palm leaves, grapes or dates and usually flavored with aniseed. It is known in Turkish as raki and in Greek as ouzo. It is forbidden like all alcoholic drinks, by the holy law of Islam but is very widely drunk in the Middle East.

Aramaic: Babylonian-Hebrew language

Arkan singular rukn: The five rukn "pillars" of Islam. (See rukn)

Arsh al-mu'mini **(A):** The throne of the true believer; the throne of one who has steadfast *iman* [absolute faith, certitude, and determination]; the throne of an *insan,* a true man who has that perfect certitude of *iman.* Allah resides within the heart which praises Him, the tongue which speaks only virtuous thoughts, the tongue which speaks the truth and praises the truth

Arsh: Literally throne. It is quite difficult to appreciate fully its exact nature. It may stand for dominion and authority and that God's ascending the Throne signifies His actual taking over the reins of the universe after having created it. Whatever the exact meaning of the expression '(Allah) ascended the Throne', the main thrust of the verse is that God is not just the creator of the universe, but is also its sovereign and ruler; that after creating the universe He did not detach Himself from, nor become indifferent to, His creation. On the contrary, He effectively rules over the universe as a whole as well as every part of it. All power and sovereignty rest with Him. Everything in the universe is fully in His grip and is subservient to His will. For a detailed discussion see **Surah** 7, n. 41 and 9:129. The throne of God; the plentitude from which God rules. The station located on the crown of the head which is the throne that can bear the weights of Allah. Allah is so heavy that we cannot carry the load without hands or legs. The *'arsh* is the only part of man that can support Allah.

AS (Alayhis Salaam): This acronym evokes a blessing and is appended to the names of the prophets who came before Muhammad. It will also be applied the mothers of those prophets. When following a woman's name, the feminine form is Alayhas Salaam

As Salamu Alaykum: The Islamic greeting literally "peace be upon you": in addition wa Rahmatullahi wa Barakatuhu means "and the mercy of God and his blessing". The response to this greeting is wa Alaykum us Salam wa Rah,atullahi wa Barakutuhu "and on you be the peace and mercy of God and His blessing

As Siraat: A bridge over hell crossed by people on Judgment Day (The Path). The bridge on which judgment of where a person's akhira (afterlife) will lie is passed.

Asabiyya: Social solidarity

Asbab An-Nazool: Circumstances of the revelations.

Asceticism: Denying oneself physical pleasures in the belief that this practice frees the body from material concerns and allows union with the divine.

Ash'ari: Orthodox theological school founded by Abu'l Hasan al Ash'ari (873-74 to 935-36) combining the literal reading of the Koran of the Hanbalis with rational argument (kalam), an approach developed by later theologians. Its most important political consequence was the doctrine that a Muslim remained a believer even when in a state of grave sin, hence that even a wicked caliph must be obeyed.

Ashab **(A):** Companions of Prophet Muhammad

Ashab al Suffah: Consisted of about three or four hundred Companions who spent most of their time in the company of the Prophet. They acquired knowledge and had dedicated themselves wholly to serving Islam.

Ashab al-A-'raf: (Heights) Will be the people who are neither righteous enough to enter Paradise nor wicked enough to be cast into Hell. They will, therefore, dwell at a place situated between the two.

Ashadd al-Jihad: Most strenuous jihad.

al-Asharatu Mubashsharun bil-Jannah or just Asharatu: Transliteration: *'Asharatul-mubashshirun or Asharatul-mubashshirune bil Jannah);* the ten companions of Muhammad who are promised paradise (only in Sunni Islam)

Asharites: Agnostics

Ashoura: Shia festival, the main commemoration of Husayn's martyrdom, killed in Najaf or Karbala, Iraq.

Ashraf **(sing.** *Sharif***):** Descendants of the Prophet Muhammad

Ashura: Arabic tenth meaning 10th of Muharim: a fasting day for Muslims. In Islam it is the day when Allah created Adam and Eve, paradise and hell the pen and life and death. Tradition has it that the Prophet Muhammad fasted on that day. An annual ritual of shias Ashura is the final day of the dramatic event of 1-10 Murram 61 AH. In Islamic history. It is the day God saved Moses and the children of Israel from the Pharaoh. The grandson of the Prophet Muhammad, Imam Hussayn sacrificed his life along with 72 of his companions on the sand dunes of Karbala. To the Shias, it is also a day on which they mourn the death of the third Shia in Karbala. They cry and weep and organize laminating programmers where they not only learn how to live a proper Islamic life and improve their spiritual self but also cry at the end of the ritual to show their true love and faith towards imam Hussayn. Tenth day of month of Muharram, held in special reverence by Shi'i Muslims since it commemorates death of Imam Husain in 680 AD at Karbala.

Ashura: Month of fasting

Ashura: Shi'is; commemorating the Battle of Karbala at which the Imam Husayn was killed on the tenth day of the month of Muharram in the year 680 ACE.

ASL: Root, origin, source, principles Aslim Taslam: Submit to Islam

Aslim Taslam: "Submit to Islam" (See dawah) (See: Ian astaslem)

Asma al-husna **(A):** The ninety-nine beautiful names of Allah. The plenitude of the ninety-nine duties of God; the *sifat* of His *dhat*, the manifestations which emerge from Him. He performs His duty when these manifestations of His essence are brought into action. Then they become His *wilayat*, the actions which stem from the manifestations of His essence. The *Asma al-husna* is the ninety-nine beautiful names of His duties. They were revealed to Prophet Muhammad in the Qur'an, and he explained them to his followers. This is a vast *bahr al-dawlah*, a very deep ocean of His grace and his limitations, infinite, and undiminishing wealth. If we go cutting one of these ninety-nine *wilayat* over and over again, taking one piece at a time, we will see ninety-nine particles revolving one around the other without touching. This applies to each one of the ninety-nine *wilayat*. This is the *Asma al-husna*. As we go on cutting, we lose ourselves in that. We die within that. How can we ever hope to reach an end of the ninety-nine? If we receive only one drop of that, it will be more than sufficient for us. The person who has touched the smallest, tiniest drop becomes a good one. These are merely His powers. If you go on cutting just one of His powers, it is so powerful that it will draw you in. That power will swallow you up, and you become the power [*wilayat*]. Then you come to the stage at which you can lose yourself within Allah; you can disappear within Allah List of God's 99 names, According to a hadith the one who enumerates them all will enter Paradise. The Beautiful Names of God, totaling ninety-nine in the canonical list but up to 300 for others; the Divine Names.

Asma wa'l sifat: The names and attributes of God, typically said to number ninety nine, contrasted with the Essence, which is God in himself, beyond name and designation.

Asma' Ul-Husna: Most beautiful names (of God).

Asr: Taken literally, signifies time age and epoch, it also signifies afternoon. The Asr prayer is one of the five obligatory prayers and is performed after the time for the Zuhr prayer ends, and before the time for the Maghrib prayer begins. The midafternoon prayer; title of the 103rd Sura of the Holy Qur'an. Also means time through the ages.

Assalaamu Alaikum: "Peace be unto you." Used upon greeting and leaving a Muslim. The Peace (salam) of God be upon you; the most frequent and important of Muslim greetings.

Assassin: (from the Arabic *hashishiyun*, 'smoker of hashish') A member of a secret sect of the Ismaili branch of Shiite Islam. It was founded by Hasan ibn al-Sabbah in 1078 to support the claim of Nizar to the Fatimid caliphate, and established a headquarters at Alamut in north-west Persia....The Mongol Hulagu took Alamut in 1256, executing the grand master of the order. Their last Syrian strongholds fell to the Mameluke Baybars in 1273. (The widely scattered Nizari branch of the Ismailis, who revere the Aga Khan, are their spiritual descendants.)

As-Sirat: The bridge by crossing which it is determined (judged) whether a person would go to heaven or hell. How a person crosses the Sirat depends on what they have done in their life and what they have believed in .

Assma' ul Husna: "The Most Beautiful Names." A list of the 99 names of God through which Muslims understand what God is like.

***Astaghfiru Allah al-'Azim* (A):** I seek forgiveness from Allah the Supreme. "God forgive me."

Astrolobe: The basic astronomical instrument used and developed by the Arabs to measure altitudes, determined the hour of day and cast horoscopes. The body suspended by a ring, its circular and composed of several interlocking disks with a central axis on which turn the "spider" (ankabut), representing the vault of the fixed stars revolving around the earth at rest, and the alidad, a flat ruler determining sines, cosines, tangents, and cotangents. Astrolabes were valid only for single latitude till al Zarqali/Azarchel (1068-91) produced generally valid astrolabes.

Atabat: Literally, 'thresholds' or 'doorways'; denoting Holy Cities of Shi'ism in Iraq; Najaf, Karbala, al-Kazimiyya, Samarra.

Atabeg: The Title given by Seljuk and Mamluk rulers to the emir appointed guardian of a crown prince. In the 12th century certain atabegs took advantage of the weakening of the Great Seljuks to make themselves independent, e.g. in Fars, Syria and northern Iraq, while in Mamluk Egypt, on the death of the Sultan Al Malik al Nasir Muhammad in 1341, there ensued a series of short reigns entirely controlled by successive atabegs in the names of his sons who had not attained their majority.

Ataqullah: "Be conscious of God's presence in your life."

Audhu billah: "I seek refuge in God" this is a paraphrase on the beginnings of the two last suras in the Qur'an.

Audhu Hillahi Min al-Shaytan al-Rajim: I seek refuge in God from the evils of the accursed Satan.

Awliya **(A) (sing.** *wali***):** The favorites of God. Those who are near to God, referring to holy men of Islam. Friends, protectors, helpers, caretaker, maintainer

Awqaf: *see* waqf(s): A charitable bequest, generally for a mosque or school, or for some persons specially nominated; religious endowments.

Awrah: The parts of the body, male or female must be covered in public but not between spouses, such as body parts of a woman that must be concealed before non related men.

Awsat: Middle

Awwal Muhammad **(A):** The first Muhammad; the beginning; the emergence of creation; the time Muhammad emerged, resonated, and pulsated within Allah

38

Saul Silas Fathi

Ayah: (Plural, **Ayat**) (Arabic) Sign, parable. In the Koran, the manifestations of God in the world. Verse from the Quran; a sign pointing to God.

Ayas: Verses within the suras; literally "signs".

Ayatollah: Literally, "miraculous sign of God," a title used by the Shi'a in Iran and latterly also in Iraq for the highest rank in their religious hierarchy. Both the title and the hierarchy are of comparatively recent origin. An even more recent development is the Title Ayatollah I Uzma literally the greatest miraculous sign of God, commonly translated Grand Ayatollah. Literally, 'sign from God'; an honorific title for senior Shi'i clerics.

Ayn al-Jam: The essence of union (of God)

Aysh: Means a sign which directs one to something important. In the Quran the word has been used in four different senses: 1) sign or indication: 2) the phenomena of the universe; 3) miracles performed by the prophets; and 4) individual units of the Book of God.

Ayyam al Tashriq: Signifies four days of the month of Dhu al Hijjah 10th through 13th

Azan: The Muslim call to prayer consisting of several religious statements.

Azeris: Also called Azeri Turks. These Turkic people speak a language that s akin to modern Turkish. In Iran they are the predominant majority in the provinces of east and west Azerbaijan with a combined population of 6.3 million in 2003.

Azhar: Resplendent

Azl: In sex, coitus interrupts

Azra'il: The proper name of the angel of death, also known as **Malikul Mawt.**

B.B.H.N.: Blessed be his name acronym for SAWS *see* P.B.U.H.

Baath "renaissance" party: Promotes pan-Arabism or Arab world unity, subscribes to socialist ideology, and seeks an independent, assertive Arab world position. Different Baath factions rule in Iraq and Syria, although Saddam and President Assad of Syria are enemies.

Baatil: see Batil

Bábism: The doctrines of a messianic Shiite Muslim sect founded in 1844 by the Persian Sayyid Ali Muhammad of Shiraz (1819-50). Known as the Báb ed-Din (the gate or intermediary between man and God), he declared himself to be the long-awaited Mahdi. For inciting insurrection by Báb was arrested in 1848 by the government and executed in 1850, his remains being interred (1909) on Mt. Carmel, Palestine. In 1863 Baha'ullah and his son Abdul Baha declared themselves the new leaders, and the religion they founded became known as Baha'ism.

Baca: Valley of…

Baghawat: Insurgency against a legitimate government

Bahimah: Signifies every quadruped animal. Bahimah thus refers to goats, sheep and cows

Bahr al-'ilm: The ocean of divine knowledge

Bai'a: Pledge

Bait al-Hikmah: House of Wisdom

Bait al-Mal: Public treasury

Baitullāh(*baytullāh*): A mosque, literally "house of God". Specifically means the Ka'aba at Makkah (Mecca).

Banat al-Lah: (Arabic) the Daughters of God; in the Koran, the phrase refers to the three pagan goddesses al-Uzza and Manat. The cult of the Daughters of God.

Banhi Isra'il: The Children of Israel.

Bani Qaynuqa: The smallest of the three Jewish tribes (smiths and craftsmen) about 700 fighting men.

Banu Harun: Sons of Aaron

Banu Nadir: Jewish tribe in Medina

Banu Qaynuqa: Jewish tribe in Medina

Banu Quaraiza: Jewish tribe in Medina

Baqa: Subsistence, permanence, remaining, contrasted with fana, annihilation, impermanence, disappearance, in Sufism the replacement of human limitations by the divine attributes in the image of which man was created. Entering the subsistence of the divine form in which Adam was created.

Barak Allahu Feekum: May Allah bless you, response to expression of thanks.

Barakah: Signifies growth and increase. The notions of elevation and greatness as well as of permanence and stability are also an essential part of the word's meaning. A form of blessing. Also spiritual wisdom and blessing transmitted from master to pupil. The special favor or divine grace which is possessed by the friends of God, or Sufi masters in particular. Blessing or benefit or grace, conferred by God on the believer.

Barzakh: A term conveying the passage from the physical world to the spiritual realm after death. "isthmus"; the intermediate realm where people are located between death and resurrection; also the World of Imagination, between the world of Spirits and the World of Bodies. "The partition." The time between death and the resurrection. The souls of the dead are in a stored state and are either dreaming pleasantly or being tormented based upon their faith and deeds while in the world. Where the soul is stored after death, awaiting the end time.

Basher: Humans literally means face but generally it refers to a personality Basirah: insight, discernment, perceptivity, deep knowledge. Sometimes used by Sufis to denote the ability to directly perceive a transcendental truth.

Bashira: Young slave woman

Basiji: Means the mobilized. A group of people who are voluntarily mobilized to go to the frontline of battle.

Basirah: Insight, discernment, perceptivity, deep knowledge.

Sometimes used by Sufis to denote the availability to directly perceive a transcendental Truth.

Basmalah: Technical name for the phrase, *bismillah arrahman ar rahim*, In the name of God, Full of Compassion, Ever Compassionate.

Bast: Expansion; contrasted with qabd, contraction, in Sufi psychology, a state of elation, joy and melting as opposed to sadness, darkness and hardening. Twelver Shi'ite institution of sanctuary in mosques and other holy places.

Batil: void

Batin: (Arabic) the inner meaning of the Koran. A **batini** is a Muslim who devotes himself to the esoteric, mystical understanding of the faith. The "hidden" dimension of existence and of scripture, which cannot be perceived by the senses or by rational thought, but which is discerned in the contemplative, intuitive disciplines of mysticism.

Batini: "Inner" dimension of Islamic principles and practices Esoteric dimensions of Islam. Path of the Sufis.

Bay'ah: Contract or oath of allegiance binding members of an Islamic sect or Sufi tariqa to their spiritual guide. An oath of allegiance to a leader, traditionally the Caliph or Imam. Loyalty.

Bay'at al-Ridwan: The pledge of good pleasure

Bayat: Oath of allegiance

Bayram: A Turkish term corresponding to the Arabic ID. The two major festivals of the Muslim year are known in Turkish as the greater and the lesser Bayram.

Bayramis: Sufi Order

Bayt Al-Hikma: School of Wisdom, Baghdad

Baytul Hikmah: "House of Wisdom." A scholarly think tank established by Caliph Ma'mun in 830 in the city of Baghdad. Most of the major translations of Greek texts into Arabic took place here.

Baytullah: "The House of God." One of the alternate names for the Ka'ah.

Bazaar: A word of Persian origin, also used in Turkish and other Islamic languages, to designate a marketplace. The Arabic equivalent is suq, sometimes transcribed souk and souq. In premodern times, the merchants and craftsmen of the marketplace, organized in guilds and corporations, played an important part and sometimes even a political role in the life of Muslim cities. They derived some strength and even independence from the fact that their leaders were not appointed from above but chosen from within the merchant community. Modernization has reduced but not eliminated that role Bazaars are found throughout the Middle East, from small villages to large cities. The grand or covered bazaar in Istanbul has more than 5,000 merchants under its rook. The labyrinths of shops and workshops are divided into areas selling the same merchandise. Acres of carpets, brassware, water pipes, handicrafts, silks, gold and silver are available.

Bazaaris: Refers to merchants, who make up a separate economic class in Iranian society

Bedouin: Bedoun [Arab.,=desert dwellers], primarily nomad Arab peoples of the Middle East, where they form about 10% of the population. They are of the same Semitic stock as their sedentary neighbors (the fellahin; see Arabs) and share with them a devout belief in Islam and a distrust of any but their own local traditions and way of life. From the Arabia Badawi, one who dwells in the desert badw. A term applied from early times to the pastoral nomads of Arabia and later of other desert areas conquered by the Arabs in the Middle East and North Africa. Pastoral nomads tribally organized, of Arabian stock, mostly now inside Arabia. The most famous of their tribes, from whom Muhammad claimed descent, was the Quraysh at Mecca who in the Mid 7th century were extensively involved in trade. The exploits of the pre Islamic Bedouin, mostly animists by religion are the theme of much early Islamic literature.

Begum (also Begam): A feminine form of the Turkish bey. It is first attested in India during the period of mogul rule and was used as a title for female members of the reigning house. In the course of time, its use was extended more generally to Muslim ladies of noble or high status. By now all married women in Muslim South Asia of what one might call the middle and upper classes are called begum. It is also used as a respectful form of address to ladies. The title is little known in Muslim lands outside the India subcontinent.

Behesht: Means "paradise," a place holding pleasure and joy.

Beit/bait: house

Bey: Originally beg, A Turkish title widely used in the Ottoman Empire and its successor states. It can be traced back in

Turkish usage to central Asia and may be derived from the old Iranian royal title bag, itself connected with the pre Islamic Iranian name of God. The same word occurs in the place name Baghdad, an old Iranian term literally meaning God Gave. In the Ottoman Empire, the term bey denoted rank and authority, the latter however subordinate to some higher authority such as a pasha. In the modern Middle East, it has become no more than a respectful form of address or reference. A similar devaluation of titles may be seen in the German Herr, the French monsieur and the Spanish senor, English sir and mister, all of which began as titles of nobility or at least gentry.

Bid'a: Innovation. A belief or practice for which the Sunna gives no precedent, generally with the implication that it is arbitrary, if not wrong. However, some innovations have been accepted, for example the codification of law and innovation, even when unacceptable, is therefore regarded as confused thinking as much as heresy. innovation in religion i.e. inventing new methods of worship. Bad Bid'ahs in Islam is considered a deviation and a serious sin by many Muslims. Blameworthy innovation.

Bid'ah sayyi'ah: Inquiry prohibited in Islam

Bin (Arabic Son): It is customary for an Arab male from the Arabian Peninsula to identify himself as the bin (son) of his father, followed by his surname, often prefixed with al (the). Those of high social rank tend to include more than one generation in the name.

Bin: son

Bint (Arabic daughter): It is customary for an Arab female to identify herself as the bint (daughter) of her father followed by his surname often prefixed with al. "Daughter of"; used in the Arabic naming system to denote relationships between father and daughter

Bismillah al-Rahman al-Rahim (A): In the name of God, Most Merciful, and Most Compassionate. *Bismillah:* Allah is the first and the last, the One with the beginning and without beginning. He is the One who is the cause for creation and for the absence of creation, the cause for the beginning and for the beginningless. *Al-Rahman:* He is the King, the Nourisher, and the One who gives food. He is the Compassionate One. He is the One who protects the creations. He is the Beneficent One. *Al-Rahim:* He is the One who redeems, the One who protects from evil, who preserves and who confers eternal bliss; the Savior. On the Day of Judgment and on the Day of Inquiry and on all days from the day of the beginning, He protects and brings His creations back unto Himself

Book of the Dead: Composite text from the walls of tombs; contains prescriptions for life in the Hereafter; preserved on papyri.

Bu (Arabic Father): Derivative of abu.

Bugis: Muslim mercenaries and traders of south-east Asia. They were enterprising seamen and traders living in villages in Sulawesi (Celebes). When Macassar fell to the Dutch (1667) they lost their livelihood. Thereafter they sought employment as mercenaries and engaged in piracy in Borneo, Java, Sumatra, and Malaya. They fought for and against the Dutch. They suffered a reverse when their leader Raja Haji was killed while assaulting Malacca

(1784), but went on to found states like Selangor and Riao, on the Malay Peninsula. Their prahus, boats with a triangular sail and a canoe-like outrigger, continued to trade throughout the archipelago.

Buraq: The creature that carried Muhammad to the Heavens and back on Isra wal Miraj. The winged horse with a human head that is supposed to have carried Muhammad from Mecca to Jerusalem and thence to Paradise on his Night Journey. The name of the heavenly steed on which the prophet rode on his nocturnal journey from Makka to Jerusalem, and then to the heavens. A winged beast ridden by Muhammad during the "Night Journey" from Mecca to Heaven (through the "Temple Mount", Jerusalem).

Burda: Not an Arabic term, means curtain in Persian. Means covering or to cover.

Burqa (also burka, bourkah): Worn in Afghanistan and parts of Pakistan. It is a black or blue body covering garment with veiled eyeholes. A robe for women that covers the body from head to toe, with only a grid over the eyes through which to see

Caliph: (Arabic khalifa, "vicar," "Successor"): Successor to Muhammad as leader of the Muslim community. The four 'orthodox' or 'rightly guided' caliphs, according to the Sunnis, are Abu-Bakr (623-4), Umar (634-44), Uthman (644-56) and Ali (656-61). For the Shi'a the first three are usurpers, and Ali was Muhammad's directly designated successor. The supreme head of the Muslim Community. Under the Umayyads the Caliph was treated principally as a secular monarch (for with the death of Muhammad Revelation had come to an end) but the Abbasids emphasized their majesty and spiritual preeminence, which was ultimately all that remained to them with the progressive delegation of power to their viziers and the political control of Baghdad first by the Buwayhids and then by the Seljuks (10th and 11th). This authority was further weakened by the proclamation of the Umayyad Caliphate in the Maghrib and then in Egypt. After the death of the last Abbasid Caliph in Baghdad (1258), a puppet Caliphate was installed in Egypt by Babyars (1261). It has been customary to dismiss it, but its influence in the Mamluk state was not negligible.

Caliphate: Formerly the central ruling office of Islam. the dominion of the chief Muslim ruler, who is regarded as a successor of Muhammad's. The political embodiment of Islamic rule. The first caliph (Arabic, *khalifa,* 'deputy of God' or 'successor of his Prophet') after the prophet Muhammad's death in 632 was his father-in-law Abu Bakr, and he was followed by Umar, Uthman, and Ali: these four are called the Rashidun (rightly guided) caliphs. When Ali died in 661 Shiite Muslims recognized his successors, the imams, as rightful possessors of the Prophets authority, the rest of Islam accepting the Umayyad dynasty. They were overthrown in 750 by the Abbasids, but within two centuries they were virtually puppet rulers under Turkish control. Meanwhile and Umayyad refugee had established an independent emirate in Spain in 756 which survived for 250 years, and in North Africa a Shiite caliphate arose under the Fatimids, the imams of the Ismailis (909-1171). After the Mongols sacked Baghdad in 1258 the caliphate, now only a name, passed to the Mameluke rulers of Egypt, and from the Ottoman conquest of Egypt in 1517 the title was assumed by the Turkish sultans, until its abolition in 1924. Those who replaced Muhammad in 632; continued until 1926, ending with the Ottoman Empire.

Calligraphy: Ornamental Arabic or other script.

Casba: Well known to moviegoers from an Arabic word which among other things means a fortress or citadel. It is sometimes used especially in North Africa, to denote the old part of a city.

Chador: A Persian word originally meaning tent, denoting a garment worn by most women in Iran when they venture out in public. It is a full length, semi circle of Fabric, open down the front, which is thrown over the head and held closed in front and conceals the figure. A chador has no hand openings or closures but is held shut by the hands or by wrapping the ends around the waist. Islamic outer garment; worn outside house.

Chemosh: God of the Moabites

Chishtiyyah: Sufi order (mysticism).

Companion(s) of the Prophet: Ar., ansar, literally helpers; those who joined him after the Hijra (q.v.) to Medina.

Copt: The name of the ancient inhabitants of Egypt from Greek and later restricted in use for Christians. In the middle ages, a residential commercial agent.

Cuneiform: A script, or rather a family of scripts, developed in the Middle East as a result of using split reeds for writing on soft clay. Incised free-hand signs were turned into groups of impressed triangles (cuneiform means wedge-shaped) by the Sumerians c. 2500 BC. Thereafter it was adapted for other languages, including Akkadian and Assyrian. All these were elaborate scripts with signs serving many different purposes; practice tablets and glossaries show that it required long training to write properly. The forms were rigidly maintained, even when inscriptions were carved on stone. About 1500 BC in Persia, alphabets of cuneiform signs were invented, eventually to be replaced by derivatives of the Phoenician alphabet.

Da'i : Propagandist or missionary, especially in Shi'ite Isma'ili movements.

Da'wah: "call or invitation" Summoning others to heed the call of God to Islam; propagation of the faith. Propaganda or missionary Dervish: Mendicant, member of a Sufi tariqa Inviting others to Islam; calling non-Muslims to the faith, to convert. Literally call, signifies an invitation to join the faith of Islam or the spreading of the message of Islam; 'call to Islam', propagation of the faith; more broadly, social welfare and missionary activities.

Dabba: A creature that Allah will release just shortly before the Last Day. It will speak to people and mark believers from nonbelievers.

Daeef: Weak

daff: A simple open air drum; the only musical instrument universally accepted among Muslims

Dahr: Time/fate

Dahri: Atheist, from the root as dahr meaning time. In Islam, atheists are seen as those who think that time only destroys, hence the term as dahriyyah for the concept of atheism.

Dai: Agent

Dajjal: An Islamic figure similar to the Antichrist, means liar or deceiver a false prophet (?) Anti-Christ. A false prophet (devil).

Dallal: Going astray

Dar al Ahd: the Ottoman Empire's relationship with its Christian tributary states.

Dar al Amn: Means house of safety, refers to the status of a Muslim living in some of the Western world.

Dar ad Dawa: a region where Islam has recently been introduced.

Dar al Harb: (Domain of War or House of War), Refers to the territory under the hegemony of unbelievers, which is on terms of active or potential belligerency with the Domain of Islam, and presumably hostile to the Muslims living in its domain. In theory, all territory outside the Dar al Islam the Land of Islam, though states might conclude truces with Muslim states against payment of tribute without actual conversionritories which did not recognize Islam were under threat of a missionary war (jihad), as were territories like 10th and 12th century Syria, which were temporarily recaptured by Non Muslims Byzantines or Crusaders.

Dar al Islam: Realm of Islam, originally those lands under Muslim rule, later applying to lands where Muslim institutions were established. The whole territory in which the law of Islam prevails, recognizing the community of the Faithful (umma), the unity of the law (sharia) and the protected status of the People of the Book (ahl al kitab, hence dhimmi). Literally, "House of Islam". Also known as dar as-salam, or the abode of peace.

Dar al Kufr: Means domain of disbelief, the term originally refers to the Quraish dominated society of Mecca between Prophet Muhammad's flight to Medina and the cities conquest.

Dar al-Hikmah: The Abode of Wisdom

Dar Al-Ilm: House of Learning; founded in early 11th century in Fatimid, Cairo.

Dar as Salam: The house of peace, a Qur'anic epithet for Paradise; a place that participates in the peace of the Divine Presence. Equivalent to dar al-Islam. House of Peace

Dar as Sulh: Domain of agreement

Dar ash Shahada: see Dar al Amn

Dar: House or realm

Darud: Blessing

Darwis: An initiate of the Sufi Path one who practices Sufism.

Da'wah: the call to Islam, proselytizing.

Dawlah (A): This has two meanings. One is the wealth of the world, or *dunya*. The other is the wealth of the grace of Allah. The wealth of Allah is the wealth of the divine knowledge known as *'ilm* and the wealth of perfect *iman*, or absolute faith, certitude, and determination

dawlati: State or national

Declaration of Faith: An oath declaring belief in Allas as the only God, and in Muhammad as His slave and messenger. Divine code of life; living in accordance with one's faith; way of life

Deen: Religion

Deewani: Islamic script; calligraphy.

Dergah: Originally, royal court, threshold, in Turkey a Sufi center

Dervish: From the Persian darvesh meaning poor indigent. A common term for Sufis of any persuasion, but particularly applied to the wandering Sufis (Qalandariyya) whose failure to belong to the established orders excited reproaches of vagrancy, heresy or vice. This is the term used to denote a member of a religious more specifically Sufi fraternity. There are many such fraternities, each professing a version of Sufi Islam, and each with its own distinctive rites and rituals. The most famous are the Mevlevi, sometimes known as the dancing or whirling dervishes. This order, founded by the great poet Jalal al Din Rumi, played a role of some important in the Ottoman Empire. Some of these orders are now strongly established in the US. They and their version of Islam are totally rejected by the Wahhabis. Islamic devotee dedicated to a life of poverty and chastity, some of whom practice whirling as part of their religious experience.

Dhabh: Means to split or pierce, to cut the throat of any creature. Dhabh is the process of killing required by Islam for legitimizing the consumption of the flesh of animals. Slaughter

Dhat: The essence of God; His treasury; His wealth of purity; His grace

Dhikr : The remembrance of God. It is a common name given to certain words in praise of God. Of the many *dhikrs*, the most exalted *dhikr* is to say, *"La ilah illa Allah* – There is nothing other than You. Only You are Allah." All the others relate to His *wilayat*, or His actions, but this *dhikr* points to Him and to Him alone. See also: *kalimah; La ilah illa Allah*

Dhikr or zikr (in Persian/Urdu): remembrance of God; spiritual exercise; Muslims believe that the primary function of prophets is to remind people of God.

Dhimmi: A member of one of the tolerated non Muslim religions, that is, those recognized by a pact, dhimma, in accordance with holy law. In return for the payment of certain taxes, notably the poll tax, or Jizya, and the acceptance of certain social, fiscal, and legal disabilities, dhimmis were permitted the practice of their own religious and large measure of autonomy in their own internal affairs. The system worked well enough in the Ottoman Empire until the 19th century when it broke down under the impact of such imported European ideas as freedom, equality and above all nationality. Second class citizenship even with an assured and protected status, was no longer acceptable and the various subject peoples the Greeks, Serbs, Bulgars, Armenians, and eventually even the Jews, created their own states. This naturally aroused resentment and suspicion in Muslim ruling circles, directed immediately against those non Muslims who remained under their rule. At the present time, in Saudi Arabia the practice of any religion other than Islam is strictly prohibited a ban that is rigorously enforced. In some other countries in the region, the non Muslim communities, steadily growing smaller by emigration have managed to achieve some sort of modus vivendi with the dominant order. Some of them look back with yearning on the good old days of dhimmitude. Second class citizenship, maintained by law, guaranteed by custom and tradition, respected by both government and people, is considerably better than no citizenship and no rights at all which is the lot of majorities and minorities alike under the rule of the tyrants that dominate so much of the Middle East at the present time. Protected person, Jews and Christians and sometimes others such as Buddhists, Sikhs, Hindus and Zoroastrians, living in an Islamic state whose right to practice their religion is tolerated under Islamic law.

Dhir: Royal decree

Dhirk: 'remembrance', Sufi practice of repeating or remembering God's name to become more conscious of God's presence.

Dhuhr: Second salat prayer; the noon prayer

Dhul Fiqar: Double-edged sword

Dhul Qina: The Man of the Veil, charismatic Yemeni warlord who led the pagan resistance to Islam in the immediate aftermath of the death of the Prophet Muhammad.

Dhulm: Transgression, going out of all bounds in moral behavior.

Dhuhr: second salat prayer

Dia: The title of the rulers of Kukia.

Dikka: A raised platform in a large mosque in front of the **mihrab (q.v.)** for cantors, to enable the congregation to keep in time with the **imam (q.v.)** in prayer.

Din **(A):** The light of perfect purity; the resplendence of perfectly pure *iman*, absolute faith, certitude, and determination. Lit.: religion, faith, or belief; The last and perfect religion given to the last Prophet of God for humankind, namely Islam; any religion that addresses the Divine. (A) the light of perfect purity; the resplendence of perfectly pure **iman,** absolute faith, certitude, and determination. Lit.: religion, faith, or belief. the core meaning of din is obedience. As a Quran technical term, din refers to the way of life and the system of conduct based on recognizing God as one's sovereign and committing oneself to obey Him. According to Islam, true din consists of living in total submission to God, and the way to do so is to accept as binding the guidance communicated through the Prophets. The pursuit of religious belief as a way of life, as opposed to the pursuit of a worldly existence.

Din al-Islam **(A):** The faith of surrender to the will of Allah

Din-I-Ilahi: Divine religion (Akbar's).

Dinar: The gold unit of the Islamic coinage. The earliest Umayyad type imitated the solidus of Heraclius but with a Muslim legend. But Abd al Malik's coinage reform of 698-88 established a standard epigraphic type of high fineness (96%-98%) and unvarying weight which was maintained without significant debasement till the 11th century, though the dinars of later dynasties tend to vary slightly in appearance.

Dirham: The silver unit of the Islamic coinage from the Rise of Islam. Initially dirhams immigrated Sasanian silver coins while adding a Kufic inscription giving the governor's name and the mint. Then after some experimentation Abd al Malik (698-99) introduced a purely epigraphic type which was to become standard. From the 11th century onwards as well documented silver famine left to the issue of base dirhams and when after the Mongol invasions silver dirhams were again struck, they differed considerably in design and weight from the earlier standard type.

Divan: At the present day this term in most languages denotes a kind of long seat or couch. Of disputed etymology, the word is probably of Persian origin, but was widely used in Arabia, Turkish and other Islamic languages with a variety of meanings. It commonly occurs in two senses one literary and the other bureaucratic or governmental. In the first sense it denotes the collected works of an author, usually a poet. In the second it was used for the written registers compiled from early Islamic times, containing administrative, financial and other relevant information. By extension, the word diwan came to be used from early times not only for the registers but also more commonly for the offices that compiled and maintained them. This no doubt gave rise to an alternative explanation of the origin of the world deriving it from the Persian dev a devil and interpretation it to mean crazy or devil possessed in presumed reference to the sound and appearance of bureaucrats. By Ottoman times, the Imperial council which in the early centuries was the central organ of the Sultan's government. We find it widely used in the related senses of a council state of the chamber in which the council met, and then of the long seat against the all, on which the councilors set. It is in the last sense that the word has come to be used in English and other European languages to denote an article of furniture. The collected short poems of a poet.

Diwan: Bureaucracy of a city or country. The medieval equivalent of a ministry dealing with taxes, land grants, pious foundations and military affairs and the means by which royal decisions formulated in the chancery (diwan al insha) were implemented. They each had their archives few of which have survived, except those of the Ottoman Empire in the Topkapi Saray in Istanbul now the Basvekalet Arsivi.

Diya: An Arabic term, usually translated blood wit for the compensation to be paid in case of homicide to the family of the victim. In the case of deliberate murder they may insist on the execution of the perpetrator. Alternatively and in cases of involuntary homicide they may accept a specified payment in goods or money as compensation. The system which dates back to pre Islamic Arabia was retained with some modifications in Islamic law and practice. The circumstances and obligations are regulated in some detail. The highest rate of diya is payable where the victim is a male free Muslim. The rate for a woman is half that of a man. The rate for a non Muslim legally present in Muslim territory is various assessed by some authorities at the rate of one third others at the rate of one half, some even at an equal rate for that of Muslims. The death of a slave must be compensated according to his replacement value. fine for unintentional murder

Dowry: Dowry, the property that a woman brings to her husband at the time of the marriage. The dowry apparently originated in the giving of a marriage gift by the family of the bridegroom to the bride and the bestowal of money upon the bride by her parents. Generally the husband has been compelled to return the dowry in case of divorce or the death of the wife when still childless. One purpose of the dowry was to provide support for the wife on the husband's death, and thus it was related remotely to the rights of dower.

Dragoman: From the Arabic tarjuman an interpreter or translator. The word, and the profession that it denotes, can be traced back to remote antiquity in the Middle East. From the beginnings of diplomatic and commercial relations between Middle Eastern rulers and European governments, both sides employed dragomans, who often played a role of some importance in negotiations. At a time when Middle Eastern Muslims knew no European languages, and few if any European Christians knew any Arabia, Persian or Turkish, the dragomans on both sides were mainly recruited from the local non Muslim minorities. At first these sometimes included Jewish refugees from Europe, who had found sanctuary in the lands of Islam. Later they were exclusively Christian and for the most part recruited from the community known as Levantines. In time the study of Middle Eastern languages in the Middle east made the services of the Levantines unnecessary and both sides were able to train and appoint translators from among their own people.

Du'a: An invocation or prayer addressed to God that is not part of the five daily prayers (salat); personal prayers or supplications; supplication, personal requests to God;

individual or spontaneous prayer. Virtuous goals

Dunya : The earth-world in which we live; the world of physical existence; the darkness which separated from Allah at the time when the light of the *Nur Muhammad* manifested from within Allah; the material world, or (excessive) concern with material, worldly goods. The physical universe as opposed to the Hereafter. Life on earth.

Eden: One of the elite Heavens.

Effendi: Often incorrectly written as effendi. Along with bey the most widely used form of address in Turkey and the Arab east at the present time, though in recent years there has been a tendency to abandon it in favor of purer Turkish or Arab designations. The term goes back to Ottoman and before that to Byzantine origins. It derives from the ancient Greek authentic, one who kills with his own hand, as distinct from one who hires or instructs others to kill that is one who is authentic. By a natural evolution authentic acquired the secondary meaning of master or ruler. Later Effendi came to be used of various dignitaries of steadily decreasing status and eventually was little more than a polite form of reference or address. In the Turkish Republic it has been formally abolished along with other Ottoman ranks and titles but remains in common use as a form of address. As a title suffixed to the name in Turkey it is applied more particularly to men of religion. In the Arab countries, in contrast it came to designate the secular literate townspeople usually dressed in European style as contrasted with the lower classes on the one hand and the men of religion on the other.

Ehtiaat: Also Ahwat. A Precaution, either obligatory or optional.

Ehtiaat: Mustahabbi: A preferred precaution.

Ehtiaat: Waajib: An obligatory precaution.

Eid al Adha (Arabic: Festival of Sacrifice): Islamic festival One of the two canonical Festivals, Eid al Adha is also known as Eid al Qurban, Persian for Sacrifice or Eid al Kabir, the major festival. It falls on 10 Dhul Hajji, the last month of the Islamic calendar when the hajj is undertaken by the faithful. The Festival of Sacrifice, which marks the end of the Hajj the annual feast day of sacrifice held on the tenth day of the Islamic month Dhu al-Hijjah, the month of pilgrimage; of Sacrifice, and the last day of the **haj**. Muslim holiday; observed at the end of the pilgrimage; the Festival of Sacrifice.

Eid al Fitr (Arabic the festival of breaking the fast): Islamic festival, One of the two canonical festivals, Eid al Fitr is also called Eid al Saghir, the Minor Festival. It falls on 1 Shawaal, which follows Ramadan the month of fasting. Festival of Charity or festival of the breaking of the fast, the end of the month of fasting, Ramadan

Eid: Holiday or festival; '**Eid al-Fitr** – observance of the end of Ramadan; '**Eid al-Adha** – observance on the last day of the **hajj** or pilgrimage to Mecca.

El Hashasheen: Shiite Muslims who believed killing the enemy was an Islamic command to be martyred; used "hashish"

El Hejhera: Immigration

El Kharij: Seventh century Islamic movement calling for return to purity of faith

El Najune Min El Narr: Rescued from hell

El-Khazrahg: Jewish clan in Arabia that was forced to convert to Islam.

Emanation: A process whereby the various grades of reality were imagined to flow from a single, primal source, which the monotheists identified as God. Some Jews, Christians and Muslims, including philosophers and mystics, preferred to use this ancient metaphor to describe the origins and mystics, preferred to use this ancient metaphor to describe the origins of life than the more conventional biblical story of an instantaneous creation of all things by God in a moment of time.

Emanuel Mufassil: The seven main beliefs of Islam listed in detail.

Emir (Arabic Amir): The title given to great military commanders (the ahl al sayf or Men of the Sword), particularly under the Seljuks, Ayyubids, Mongols and Mamluks. With the development of the iqta system they became military governors of large provinces while holding high positions at court-Grand Chamberlain, Keeper of the Wardrobe, Cupbearer etc. The government was carried out by the vizier and his staff or the ulama the ahl al qalam, or Men of the Pen. One who gives amr (command); commander; a prince, a Muslim ruler, chief or commander. The political leader of an Islamic community. In the 1990s, the term has been applied to the military leaders of Islamist organizations.

Emirate: A Muslim territory ruled by an emir (Arabic *amir*, 'lord' or 'prince'), who often united civil and military authority.

Depending on the strength of the Caliphate, an emir might be either a diligent subordinate, subject to supervision and removal, as under the early Abbasids, or a virtually independent princeling, able to defy his nominal master. The term *amir* could also be applied to a specific office such as commander-in-chief of the armies (*ami al-umara*) or leader of the pilgrimage (*amir al-hajj*). It was also applied as a courtesy title to descendants of Muhammad and is the origin, via medieval Italian, of the English title 'admiral'.

Esa: The Islamic name for Jesus.

Ethiaat Mustahabbi: A preferred precaution

Ethiaat Waajib: An obligatory precaution. also ahwat, a precaution, either obligatory or optional

Eve: Adam's wife in the Garden of Eden; God's first created woman.   Adam's   wife,   created from his body.

Fajarah: Wicked evil doers, plural of Fajir

Fajr: Morning, as in the morning prayer. The time of the day when there is light in the horizon before sunrise; the predawn prayer

Fakir (Faqir): Islamic holy men who vow to live a life of poverty and that rivaled the Abbasid dynasty; poor in spirit.

Falah: Deliverance, salvation, well being

Falak: Plural aflak means celestial body and the orbit of a celestial body

Fallah or Fellah: An Arabic word, possibly of Aramaic origin, meaning peasant. The Arabic plural is fellahin.

Falsafah: (Arabic) philosophy. The attempt to interpret Islam in terms of ancient Greek rationalism. philosophy, the method ad content of Greek philosophy which was brought into Islam. A person who tried to interpret Islam through rationalist philosophy was called a faylasuf

Fana: (Arabic) annihilation. The ecstatic absorption in God of the Sufi mystic. Sufi term meaning extinction, to die to this life while alive. Having no existence outside of God annihilation in God (Sufi's) A Sufi mysticism denoting a temporal union with the beloved (God).

Fana: see baqa

Fana: The utter effacement and dissolution of "otherness", the full realization of the "no God but God" (Tawhid).

Faqih: A specialist in fiqh that is to say Islamic jurisprudence. A faqih is thus a scholar of the Shari'a, the holy law of Islam; beggar, recluse; a follower of Sufism who has embraced poverty or detachment from worldly goods. Islamic jurisprudent One who practices fiqh Arabic knowledge the term for jurisprudence the science of religious law in Islam. A jurisprudent; a supreme religious eminence.

Faqir: A Sufi term for a "beggar" who has embraced poverty. (Fakir) poor in spirit.

Al-Faraj: the return of the Shia Mahdi

Fard, plural Fara'id furud: a religious duty, or an obligatory action: *praying 5 times a day*
is *fard.* Neglecting a fard will result in a punishment in the hereafter. (See wajib)

Fard ayn: Obligatory on every individual Muslim to aid in any way he can; a religious duty, or an obligatory action, praying five times a day is a fard, neglecting a fard with result in a punishment in the hereafter; compulsory act or practice, such as fasting Ramadan.

Fard bi al-Kifayah: Signifies a collective duty of the Muslim community so that if some people carry it out no Muslim is considered blameworthy, but if no one carries it out all incur a collective guilt. An obligation of the Muslim community as a whole from which some are freed if others take it up such as for jihad.

Fasiq: Anyone who has violated Islamic law, usually refers to one whose character has been corrupted; transgressor, evil-doer, disobedient. For further elaboration see Surah 2

Fasting: Refraining from food, water, and foul behavior from the dawn prayer to the sunset prayer.

Fat'h (Fatiha): Opening. Victory of Hudaybiyah opening

Fatiha: The opening chapter of the Koran which is therefore often splendidly illuminated. It has come to be recited also as an occasional prayer, particularly on passing the tombs of learned or pious men, though orthodox Islam rejects the idea of prayers for the dead. The short opening sura of the Quran which begins "in the name of God the Merciful the Compassionate. Praise be to God the Lord of the Worlds"

These words hold important place in Muslim liturgies and forms the core of the Salat. "The Opening One," the first sura of the Holy Qur'an.

Fatwa: A formal opinion or judgment delivered by an expert in the *Shari'a*. A ruling given in answer to a question on a point of Islamic law. It is issued by a qualified religious authority known as a mufti. The modern used of the phrase to issue a fatwa as an equivalent to the American to put out a contract, is entirely without precedent in Islamic history, doctrine or law. Its use in this sense seems to date from February 1989, when the Ayatollah Khomeini the highest Islamic religious authority in Iran, issued a fatwa sentencing Salman Rushdie, the author of the Satanic verses and also those involved in its publication that were aware of its contents to death. An even broader reinterpretation of the term occurs in the fatwa issued by Osama Bin Laden and his associates in February 1998, to the effect that to kill Americans and their allies both civil and military is an individual duty of every Muslim who is able in any country where this is possible. As indicated the use of fatwa in this sense is an innovation of the late 20th century CE, without precedent in Islamic history, culture or law. In the past it was not unknown for a mufti to issue a fatwa ratifying a death sentence or a declaration of war, but this was issued by a properly constituted chief mufti; in the former case normally after a properly conducted trial in the latter in response to a request from state authority. religious opinion, legal opinion

Fawahish: Applies to all those acts whose abominable character is self-evident. In the Qur'an all extra-marital sexual relationships, sodomy, nudity, false accusation of unchastely, and taking as one's wife a woman who had been married to one's father, are specifically reckoned as shameful deeds. In **Hadith**, theft, taking intoxicating drinks and begging have been characterized as **fawahish** as have many other brazenly evil and indecent acts.

Fayd I aqdas: Most Holy Effusion; Ibn Arabi's term for God's awareness of himself and of all that will ever be

Faylasuf: (Arabic) philosopher. Used of Muslims and Jews in the Islamic empire who were dedicated to the rational and scientific ideals of **Falsafah (q.v.).**

Fedayeen: The plural of an Arabia word meaning one who is ready to sacrifice his life for the cause. It was used by a political religious terrorist group in Iran in the 1940s and 1950s. After an unsuccessful attempt on the life of the Prime Minister in 1955, the movement was suppressed and the leaders were executed. The term was revived by the militant wing of the Palestine Liberation Organization and since the 1960s has been their common self description.

Feddan: Area measurements used in the Arab Middle East; 1 feddan = 4 donums = 1.038 acres.

fellah: Peasant

Female Circumcision: Tribal, not Muslim tradition

Fez: A red cap resembling an upside down flowerpot named after the city in Morocco where it was first manufactured. It was introduced into Turkey in the early 19th century, while the turban was restricted to religious personages. It was abolished in Turkey in 1928, but survived for sometime longer in the ex Ottoman Arab provinces where it was known as tarbush; conical hat that tapers to a flat crown.

Fi Amanillah: May Allah protect you, Said when a person departs.

Fi sabil Allah: (in the way of Allah) Is a frequently used expression in the Qur'an which emphasizes those good acts should be done exclusively to please God. Generally the expression has been used in the Qur'an in connection with striving or spending for charitable purposes. Arabic for "for the pleasure of Allah"; for the sake of Allah, common Islamic expression for performing acts such as charity or Jihad and for qatla (fighting mortal combat for the sake of Allah.)

Fikr (A): Contemplation; meditation; concentration of God; thought, reflection, meditation; in Sufism the complement of dhikr

Fiqh: Islamic jurisprudence, Fiqh includes all aspects of religious, social, and political life, covering not only ritual and religious observances, the law of inheritance, property and contracts and criminal law, but also constitutional law, laws concerning state administration and the conduct of war. Islamic jurisprudence became established within a century of the emergence of Islam in AD 622. Jurisprudence built around the Shariah by custom. Literally means deep understanding refers to understanding the Islamic laws. Knowledge acquired by studying the book of revelation and the book of nature.

Firdaws (A): The eighth heaven. If we can cut away the seven base desires known as the *nafs ammarah*, what remains will be Allah's qualities, actions, and conduct, His gracious attributes, and His duties. If man can make these his own and store them within his heart, then that is *firdaws*. That is Allah's house, the limitless heaven. That will be the eighth heaven, Allah's house or infinite magnitude and perfect purity.

Fi sabil Allah: for the sake of Allah; common Islamic expression for performing acts such as charity or Jihad and for 'qatlu' (fighting in mortal combat for the sake of Allah)

Fisq: Transgression; consists of disobedience to the command of God.

Fitan: Sedition, in application to the lay authority.

Fitnah: Has been used in the Quran in two meanings. It refers, firstly, to persecution, to a situation in which the believers are harassed and intimidated because of their religious convictions. Secondly, it refers to the state of affairs wherein the object of obedience is other than the One True God. Temptation, trial. Specifically, the term is used to describe the civil wars that rent the Muslim community apart during the time of the **rasbidun (q.v.)** and the early Umayyad period. Temptation or trial, the name given to the civil wars which broke out within the expanding Muslim empire during the first 200 years after Muhammad's death. Trial or punishment Chaos and disorder.

Fitoor: Evening meal after the daytime fasting. the evening meal during Ramadan

Fitr: Breaking the fast

Fitrah: An inborn, natural predisposition toward God, which exists at birth in all human beings; nature as originally created by God, rooted in tawhid; innate disposition towards virtue, knowledge and beauty. Muslims believe every child is born with fitrah. The inner moral compass that all humans are born with. People can become influenced by it to seek God, or they can consciously bury it under a load of sin and denial. The Islamic belief that children are born with a natural pre-disposition toward God.

Funduq: (from the Byzantine Greek, pandokeion): An inn, though funduq plans are rarely distinguishable from khans. Foreign merchants particularly the Pisans, Genoese, Amalfitans. Florentines and Venetians, each had their own funduq, a factory which housed the colony and its archives, a church, and the central depots of goods in which they specialized.

Fuqaha: Medieval jurists

Furqan: Signifies that which enables one to distinguish between true and false; between real and fake. The criterion of right and wrong and true and false for example, the Quran as furqan. A sign of salvation.

Furud (sing. *fard*): The five *furad* refers to the five pillars of Islam: *Iman*, or absolute faith, prayer, charity, fasting, and *hajj*, or holy pilgrimage

Fusha: Modern standard Arabic; the language of the Qur'an.

Futuhat: Revelation

Futuwwah: A corporate group of young urban men, formed after the twelfth century, with special ceremonies of initiation, rituals and sworn support to a leader that were strongly influenced by Sufi **(q.v.)** ideals and practices. The Muslim code of battlefield honors that Europeans copies and labeled chivalry. Guild

Futuwwat: Spiritual chivalry, magnanimity; a general designation for good character; Muslim chivalric code.

Fuwaysiqah: vermin, evil from the root fasaqa meaning to deviate from the right way

Gabriel: Gabriel is the single most important angel in the Islamic tradition. According to Islam, Gabriel appeared before Muhammad while he was meditating in a cave. Gabriel then recited the Quran, verse by verse, commanding Muhammad to memories each line and spread it to others. The Quran is believed to be a series of quotes directly from God to Gabriel and onto Muhammad. This explains the Muslim emphasis on the actual spoken word of the Quran and why all prayers must be said in the original Arabic. In Christianity, Gabriel is believed to be one of God's archangels. Some writings say there were three such higher-ranking angels, including Michael and Raphael. Other say there were seven. Gabriel makes several appearances in Christian tradition to relay God's messages. Gabriel appears before Zacharias and tells him that John the Baptist, a predecessor of Christ, will be born to Elizabeth. Gabriel also appears before Mary to tell her that she will give birth to Jesus. This interaction with Mary is known as the Annunciation. In Judaism, Gabriel interacts twice with Daniel. The first time, after Daniel has seen a vision from God that he cannot understand, God sends Gabriel to help him interpret. The second time, Gabriel appears before Daniel and predicts the end of the Jews' exile in Babylon.

Gamaa/jamaa: Literally "society or group" al gamaa al Islamiyya is the name adopted by a number of political Islamic groups and movements group, society

Genie: The common English spelling of the Arabic term jinn. According to Muslim belief jinn are one of the three groups of intelligent beings created by God, the other two being angels and humans. Humans are made of dry clay, angels of light, jinn of fire. Like humans they may qualify for salvation or damnation, some destined for heaven, others for hell. Jinn cannot be perceived by human senses, unless they choose to reveal themselves. This they can do in various different forms. There is an extensive and varied folklore concerning the jinn in different parts of the Islamic world. They also figure prominently in the Koran.

Ghafara: To forgive, to cover up. A characteristic of God

Ghaflah: Heedlessness, forgetfulness of God, indifference original sin.

Ghaib: Unseen and transcendent, hence al ghaiba the occultation of Hidden Imams in Shiite doctrine.

Ghanimah: spoils of war, booty.

Ghasbi: Possessed unlawfully

Ghatafan: The pagan Arabian tribe that, along with the Quraysh, laid siege to Medina in the Battle of the Trench

Ghayb: The unseen, unknown

Ghazi: Warrior. Turk., originally one who took part in a **ghazzu,** or tribal raid; later one who fought in Holy War against unbelievers; a title for a war leader. Raiders; enemies of the Byzantines.

Ghazu: (Ghazwah) Originally, the "raids" undertaken by Arabs in the pre-Islamic period for booty. Later a ghazi warrior was a fighter in a holy war for Islam; often the term was applied to organized bands of raiders on the frontiers of the Dar al-Islam **(q.v.).** Raid (robberies were not considered immoral).

Ghulat: (adjective, ghuluww): The extreme speculations. Adopted by the early Shii Muslims **(q.v.),** which overstressed some aspects of doctrine. Exaggerators Exaggeration, the over emphasis of one aspect of doctrine to the point where the whole edifice of the Sunna is undermined. Hence, Ghulas or extremists.

Ghurba: Exile our situation in this world, distant from our true home with God

Ghusl: Bath, shower, washing; required before prayer; normally done after intimate sexual contact. full ablution of the whole body. Ghusl janaba is the mandatory shower after having sexual discharge. a full bath ablution

Gnanam: Divine luminous wisdom; grace-awakened wisdom. If man can throw away all the worldly treasures and take within him only the treasure called Allah and His qualities and actions, His conduct and behavior, if he makes Allah the only treasure and completeness for him – that is the state of *gnanam*

Gog and Magog: 2 tribes who will ravage the earth on the Day of Resurrection.

Grand Vizier: Wazir in the Ottoman Empire

Gulsheniy: Sufi Order

Hadath akbar: major ritual impurity which requires Niyyat for cleaning.

Hadath asghar: minor ritual impurity

Hadha min fadhle Rabbi: Qur'anic expression and phrase meaning this is by the Grace of my Lord.

Hadi: A guide, one who guides; a Muslim name for God is the Guide or Al Hadi

Hadith qudsi: A divine transmission directly revealed to Prophet Muhammad without Gabriel as an intermediary; a saying of Muhammad in which extra Qur'anic words of God are quoted. Sacred traditions.

Hadith: (Arabic narrative): sayings and doings of the Prophet Muhammad the original term Al Hadith meaning The Tradition an account of the words and deeds of the Prophet Muhammad is now used without Al with the spread of Islam after the Prophet Muhammad's death in AD 632. The result was the hadith, books of traditions, each tradition described by text and the chain of authority, going back to the original source. Some 2,700 acts and sayings of the Prophet were collected and published in six canonical works, called Al Hadith, the first collection being by Muhammad al Bukhari AD 870. Reports or traditions containing the statements made by Prophet Muhammad; eyewitness accounts of his actions as well as his endorsement and approval of other people's actions; transmitted by his Companions, they collectively define his Sunnah, or exemplary conduct. Traditions or sayings attributed to Muhammad in the writings of his contemporaries and referred to for authoritative precedent in interpreting the Qur'an.

Hadith Mashhoor: Well-known hadith; a hadith which reported by one, two or more companions from the Prophets or from another companion, but has later become well-known and transmitted by an indefinite number of people during the first and second generation of Muslims.

Hadra: Presence of God, Sufi ceremony.

Hafiz: "Guardian." A person who has memorized the entire Qur'an by heart. One who has committed the complete Qur'an to memory. One of the ninety-nine attributes of Allah, meaning "the Guardian." Someone who knows the Quran by heart, literal translation= memorizer or Protectors One who preserved; one who memorized the entire Qur'an.

Hagar: Abraham's second wife; Ishmael's mother; and Egyptian maiden. In the Bible, she is the wife of Abraham and the mother of Abraham's son Ishmael (in Arabic Ismail), who became the father of the Arab peoples. Hence Hagar is revered as one of the matriarchs of Islam and remembered with especial reverence in the ceremonies of the hajj pilgrimage to Mecca.

Haid: Menstruation

Hajj: (fifth pillar of Islam): the annual pilgrimage to Makkah required of all Muslims at least once in their lifetime. After **haj** the pilgrim is given the title **haji**. A pilgrimage; the fifth *fard*, or obligatory duty, in Islam. "Do this duty wearing the *kafan*, the shroud, like one who has died to the world. Give a share of your wealth to those who are poor. If you have a wife and children, divide your wealth among them. Even the inner desires must be surrendered – all of the self must die for the *hajj*." (Arabic setting out) the fifth pillar of Islam, hajj is decreed by the Quran, And pilgrimage to the House of Allah is incumbent upon people for the sake of Allah, upon everyone who is able to undertake the journey to it. In 2001 of the two million pilgrims, 1,364,000 were foreign Muslims, the rest Saudi. Men who have performed the hajj may take the title al-haj, women al-haja.

Hajj al Ifrad: At Miqat, declare intention for Hajj only. Maintain Ihram garments up to the Day of Sacrifice. No offering is required from him.

Hajj al Qiran: al miqat declare intention to perform both Hajj and Umrah together. After throwing the Jamrah of Al Aqabah and getting hair shaved or cut that take off his Ihram garments and sacrifice. No offering is required from him.

Hajj al Tamattu: performing Umrah during the Hajj season, and on the Day of Tarwiah a pilgrim gets into the state of Ihram for Hajj. Before making Umrah, approach the Miqat and declare the intention. End by sacrificing an animal.

Hajjaj: Pilgrim, one who has made the Hajj

Hajji: A Muslim who made the Hajj to Mecca, a title of great honor.

Hakim: A ruler's or gubernatorial title

Hakimiya: Islamic sect Hakimiya is the term used for those who followed the Fatimid Caliph al Hakim. See Druzes. Sovereignty

Halal **(A):** That which is permissible or lawful according to the commands of God and which conforms to the word of God. This relates to both food and to divine knowledge, or '*ilm*. What is permitted by divine decree. An Arabic word meaning lawful, permitted, according to the holy law of Islam. It is thus the converse of haram, unlawful, forbidden. These two terms relate to the whole range of the holy law, but their most common everyday usage is in connection with food and drink. Islam like Judaism and unlike Christianity, regulates elaborately what practicing believers are permitted or forbidden to eat and drink. Thus for example, Islam totally prohibits intoxicants. This was usually understood to mean alcoholic drinks, but has at various times and in various places been extended to include hallucinatory drugs and even tobacco. Allowed food; not prohibited (kosher)

Halaqa: A gathering or meeting for the primary purpose of learning about Islam

Halif Al-Fudul: The League of the Virtuous.

Halimah Bint Abu Dhuayb: Foster mother of Muhammad, of the Hawazin clan of the Beni Saad tribe of Bedouin.

Hallaj: Tanner, a saint of the poor

Halq: Shaving of the head, particularly associated with pilgrimage to Mecca

Halveti: A Sufi order, prominent in Turkey

Hamasa: Hamasa [Arab.,=valor], one of the great anthologies of Arabic literature. It was gathered together in the 9th cent. by Abu Tammam when he was snowbound in Hamadan, where he had access to an excellent library. There are 10 books of poems, classified by subject. Some of them are selections from long poems. This is one of the treasuries of early Arabic poetry, and the poems are of exceptional beauty. A later anthology by the same name was compiled by the poet al-Buhturi (c.820-897). The term had been used in modern times to mean heroic epic.

Hamula: An Arabic term for the extended family usually applied to a group of people descended from a common ancestor. The duration of the Hamula was normally from five to seven generations. In traditional society, the Hamula usually formed a territorial group, cultivating adjoining plots of land, and cooperating economically as a matter of course and otherwise when needed. They were bound together by strong ties of loyalty, reinforced by the common practice of marrying within the Hamula, usually cousins. The hamula formed a single group with regard to the blood wit. Family honor and social obligation alike required members of the Hamula to help each other when possible and to avenge each other when necessary. Thus, when a member of a Hamula obtained a position of power or authority, he was expected to use it to help his fellow members of the family. In terms of Western values, this might be described as nepotism. In terms of traditional values, it was the fulfillment of a social and moral obligation. Not favoring relatives but failing to do so would be seen as an offense. The pace of modern life has often weakened and sometimes broken the Hamula but the system and still more its values have by o means disappeared. A group of descendents from a common ancestor, usually from five to seven generations.

Hanafi Code: Sunni Islamic legal school The Hanafi Code is the school. The Hanafi Code is the school of the Sharia founded by Abu Hanifa al Numan AD 699-767 an Iranian merchant scholar based on Kufa. Once they had usurped the Caliphate from the Mamelukes and established an Islamic empire (1517-1918), the Hanafi doctrine became the official code. It has continued to enjoy official status even in those former Ottoman territories where the majority of local Muslims follow a different school.

Hanafis: A follower of the school of Abu Hanifa al Muhammad 'man; a school of Islamic jurisprudence which advocates tolerance of other beliefs and is generally moderate on issues like women's rights and religious observance. Referring to the Sunni Legal madhhab ascribed to Abu Hanifa. School of law founded by Abu Hanifah (d. 767). This school is dominant in many countries that formed part of the Turkish Empire, and in India. School of law founded by Abu Hanifa (died 767) which was particularly influential in the Mashriq, the Great Seljuks, the Mamluks, the Ottomans and probably the Anatolian Seljuks as well were all solidly Hanafi. The school is normally regarded as the most favorable to the development of Islamic economics commercial partnership, the rules governing permissible investment and the theory of waqf ahli a family trust which was also a pious foundation all owe much to Hanafi influence. A school of jurisprudence created by Abu Hanafi, most tolerant of differences and opinions.

Hanbali Code: Sunni Islamic legal school The Hanbali Code is the school of the Sharia founded by Ahmad ibn Hanbal AD 780-855. Opposed to the legal superstructure built upon the Quran and the Sunna. Hanbal argued that a legal decision must be reached by referring directly to the Quran and the Sunna. Tmaya's views were well received by the Mameluke caliphs (1250-1517) in Cairo. During the subsequent Ottoman Empire, Muhammad ibn Abdul Wahhab (1703-87), a Najdi cleric, was inspired by Hanbal and Taimiya. In 1745 he formed an alliance with the ruler of Najd, Muhammad ibn Saud who adopted the Wahhabi doctrine. One of the four recognized schools of law in Sunni Islam, established by Ibn Hanbal (d. AD 855); followed, in particular, by Ibn Abdul-Wahhab in the eighteenth century, and therefore dominant in modern Saudi Arabia.

Hanbalis (School of theology): Followers of the Islamic scholar Ahmad ibn Hanbal, and to Sufi mysticism though many of his followers practiced both. It was particularly important in 11th century Baghdad under the Great Seljuks and then in 12th century Syria. Its influence later declined though the severity of the celebrated scholar Ibn Taymiyya (died 1328) in Mamluk Egypt ultimately inspired Wahhabism the present rite of Saudi Arabia. Hanbalism, is chiefly known for its literalism, the doctrine that the dicta of the Koran must be believed and obeyed to the very letter.

Hanbalite: One of the four juridical schools of Sunni Islam, prominent in Saudi Arabia characterized by extreme rigor and a literal interpretation of the holy texts; has had a strong influence on the Islamist movement; one of the four juridical schools of Sunni Islam, prominent in Turkey and India

Hanbalite: Theologian

Hanif: one of the pious believers before Muhammad, not Christians or Jews, who submitted to God's oneness. True believer, a term used to describe those Arabs who were monotheists before the revelation of the Quran. Monotheists.

Hanifiyyah: The religion of Abraham.

Haqiqah: Esoteric truth which transcends human and theological limitations; reality, truth, God as the Supreme Reality and the goal of the Tariqah Reality.

Haqq: Truth, reality, right, righteousness, al haqq is one of the 99 names of God

Haraka: Pointing. The use of signs above and below the line to indicate short vowels in Arabic, Persian and Turkish. It is de riguer in all late copies of the Koran. Haraka should be distinguished from tashkil the addition of dots or strokes to differentiate consonants and oblique cases. Such dots might be thought essential for legibility but they were nevertheless often emitted by fair copyists.

Haram: That which is forbidden by truth and forbidden by the warnings or commands of God. For those who are on the straight path, *haram* means all the evil things, the actions, the food, and the dangers that can obstruct the path Ar., forbidden, sacrosanct; thus the holy places of Mecca, Medina and Jerusalem; and for Shi'ites Karbala, Najaf and others; likewise women's quarters in a dwelling; in Aden, a drinking saloon. What is forbidden by divine decree.

Harb: War, in Islamic doctrine, land of infidels where it is legal to wage jihad

Harbi: A non-Muslim living in Dar al-Harb.

Harem/Harim: The private parts of a house or palace inhabited by the women of the family hence inaccessible to adult males. A sacred place, sanctuary, forbidden area; the private rooms of a house; the women's quarters. The secluded woman's quarters of an old style Turkish or other Muslim house. The harem included wives and concubines, sometimes also female relatives and the servants in former times, slaves, including eunuchs, who attended and guarded them.

Harkat: Movement

Hasan: Good, beautiful, admirable. Also a categorization of a hadith's authenticity as acceptable.

Hasana: Good deed.

Hashimite: A descendent of Hashim the great grandfather of the Prophet. Though not necessarily directly descended from the Prophet, the Hashimites are his kinsmen, and this title was claimed by a number of dynasties, notably the Abbasid caliphs of Baghdad and the former ruling house of the Hijaz and its descendants in Iraq and Jordan is the Hashimite Kingdom of Jordan

Hasmala: An expression of faith before every sura: "In the name of God, the merciful, the compassionate" (Bi-smi Allah al-rahum, al-rahim...)

Hawaa: Vain or egotistical desire: individual passion, impulsiveness

hawala: Trustworthy hayat: life

Hawazin: Muhammad's enemies

Hawsh: In Egyptian Muslim funerary practice an unroofed enclosure, sometimes with annexed kitchen or reception rooms attached, containing families tombs. Some were on a grand scale like the hawsh of the Abbasid Caliphs in Cairo, with seven mihrabs in its great qibla wall. In Egypt funerary enclosures are a survival of Ptolemaic or even Paranoiac practice. They are now uncommon elsewhere but certainly existed in 10th century Shiraz, well away from Egyptian influence.

Hawwa: Eve, Adam's wife The name for Eve in Islam.

Haya: Life in general.

Haya: Modest, shy, opposite of arrogant.

Hayah: The plenitude of man's eternal life; the splendor of the completeness of life; the *ruh*, or the soul, of the splendor of man's life

Hayah Muhammad **(A):** Life of Muhammad

Hayat ad-Dunya: The life of this world.

84

Saul Silas Fathi

Hayat: Life

Hayf **(A):** A wrong; a harm; damage; injustice; having faults

Hayr: Walled parkland in which wild animals roamed, which was an amenity of large Islamic palaces, Qasr al Hayr al Gharbi and Qasr al hayr al Sharqi in Syrian the Jawsaq al Khaqani at Samarra and the 10th century Abbasid palace at Baghdad are examples.

Hayy ibn Yaqzan: Alive son of the Awake, a character in a story by Avicenna and elsewhere representing the fully actualized intelligence of the sage

Hazrat: Presence, title given to respected persons

Heaven: Heaven, blissful upper realm or state entered after death; in Western monotheistic religions it is the place where the just see God face to face (sometimes called the beautiful vision). In Judaism, heaven is pictured as the abode of God to which he ultimately welcomes the general resurrection the body of a Christian will be glorified and reunited forever with the soul in heaven. The Roman Catholic church teaches that before entering heaven many souls must pass through purgatory to be made ready. In Islam, the Qur'an describes heaven in graphically idyllic terms, replete with fleshly delights; but Islam also has a strong mystical tradition which places these heavenly delights in the context of the ecstatic awareness of God. In Zoroastrianism, the souls of the deceased must pass over the Bridge of the Requiter, which widens of joy and light. In both Hinduism and Buddhism, existence is considered cyclical, making the rewards and pleasures of heaven a desirable but temporary experience; the higher objective is often conceived as a release from any form of rebirth.

Hegira/Hijra: The emigration of Muhammad from Mecca to Medina in September 622. The hijra era is however reckoned from the first day of the lunar year in which it occurred mainly 16 July 622. (Arabic, Ihijra,I 'exodus', 'migration', or 'breaking of ties') Muhammad's secret departure from Mecca in 622, accompanied by Abu Bakr, to live among the people of Yathrib, later, Medina, thus founding the first Muslim community. Under the second caliph, Umar, this key event in the history of Islam was chosen as the starting point for the Muslim calendar. Arabic hijra. The exodus of Muhammad and his followers to Medina (Yathrib) in 622, following persecution in Mecca. Also called Hijra.

Hejaz: The Red Sea coastal plain of the Arabian peninsula. The region has immense historical and cultural importance as the cradle of Islam and the site of the holy cities of Mecca and Medina. Under the Ottoman Empire the Hejaz was opened up through the improvement of communications: first the construction of the Suez Canal, then the opening of the Pilgrim Railway (1908), which linked Medina with Damascus. Following the 1916 Arab Revolt, which began in the region, and the subsequent fall of the Ottoman Empire, Hussein Ibn Ali became King of independent Hejaz. He subsequently abdicated (1924) in favor of his son, Ali, who also abdicated (1925) in the face of a Wahhabi invasion. The Wahhabi leader Ibn Saud, the sultan of Najd, assumed the title of King of Hejza (1926) before uniting more of the Arabian Peninsula under his control to form the kingdom of Saudi Arabia in 1932.

Hell: (HELLFIRE), In Western monotheistic religions, eternal abode of souls damned by the judgment of God. The souls in hell are deprived forever of the sight of God. The punishment of hell is generally analogized to earthly fire. A constant feature is Satan or Lucifer (also known as Iblis in Islam), considered the ruler of hell. Among ancient Jews, Sheol or Tophet was conceived as a gloomy place of departed souls where they are not tormented but wander about unhappily. The ethical aspect apparently developed gradually, and Sheol became like the hell of Christianity. Gehenna, in the New Testament, which drew its name from the Vale of Hinnom, was certainly a place of punishment. Many Christian churches now regard hell more as a state of being than a place. In Zoroastrianism, the souls of the dead must cross the Bridge of the Requiter, which narrows for the wicked so that they fall into the abyss of horror and suffer ceaseless torment. In Buddhism, hell is the lowest of six levels of existence into which a being may be reborn depending on that being's karmic accumulations. In Arabic Jahannum: According to the Koran, the damned will be in a fire which will burn their faces until their lips peel off. It will burn their skin and each time the skin is burned, they will be given a new skin so they may continue to feel the pain. Their drink will be boiling water which shreds their guts. Boiling water will also be poured over them. They will be clad in garments of fire and beaten with Iran rods. Hypocrites will be in the lowest level of hell.

Henna: Coloring applied mostly to a bride's hands.

Hezb-I-Islami: Party

Hezbollah: (Arabic Party of Allah): Lebanese political religious movement that has been accused of terrorism. More a movement than a party, Hezbollah emerged under the leadership of Shaikh Muhammad Hussein Fadlallah, a Shia cleric after the Israeli invasion of Lebanon in June 1982, primarily to offer resistance to the Israeli occupation. It was the brainchild of Ali Akbar Mohtashemi, the Iranian ambassador to Syria from 1982-83. Though unsympathetic to its religious militancy, Syrian President Hafiz Assad found the party a suitable instrument to pressure Israeli and South Lebanon Army, troops in Israel's self declared security zone in southern Lebanon. The next month Hezbollah joined the front formed to confront the government of Gen. Michel Aoun, the Maronite army commander. It criticized the Taif Accord as perpetuating the old system, with its downgrading of Shias, now the largest single sect in Lebanon. In late 1991, a three way swap, involving 450 Lebanese and Palestinian detainees under the Israelis, seven dead or captured Israeli servicemen and the remaining Western hostages, ended Hezbollah's involvement in hostage taking. It won eight of the 27 seats reserved for Shias in the 1992 parliamentary elections. in the 2000 parliamentary poll, the Hizbollah-Amal alliance won all twenty three seats in the South and Nabatiya governorate and performed equally well in the Beqaa Valley. Means "the party of Allah". It is one of the leading political parties in Iran. the Party of God; a Shi'a militia group in southern Lebanon, supported by Iran (1980); murdered 241 U.S. Marines in Beirut in 1983 (suicide bomber).

Hidayah: Guidance from God

Hijab: *(Arabic: cover or screen)*: *see* Islamic dress; a veil that fully covers the hair, or more broadly, the modest dress that is required of Muslim women by the sharia

Hijabah: Refers to the function of keeping the key of the Ka'bah, which has traditionally been considered a matter of great honor in Arabia.

Hijar: Flight of the Prophet Muhammad

Hijra: Muhammad and his followers emigration from Mecca to Medina. Literally migration. This holiday marks the beginning of the Muslim New Year on the first day of the month of Muharram. Sometimes written Hegir, a term used for the migration of the Prophet from Mecca to Medina in the year 622 CE according to most accounts on September 20. The Muslim calendar dates from the Hijra more precisely from the beginning of the Arab year in which the hijra took place.

Hijri Calendar: The Islamic calendar or Muslim calendar or Hijri calendar is a lunar calendar based on 12 lunar months in a year of 354 or 355 days, used to date events in many Muslim countries [concurrently with the Gregorian calendar], and used by Muslims everywhere to determine the proper day on which to celebrate Islamic holy days and festivals. Its first year was the year during which the Hijra, i.e. the emigration of the Prophet of Islam, Muhammad from Mecca to Medina, occurred. Each numbered year is designated either H for Hijra or AH for the Latin anno Hegirae [in the year of the Hijra]. A limited number of years before Hijra [BH] are used to date events related to Islam, such as the birth of Muhammad in 53 BH. The Islamic calendar is not to be confused with the lunar calendar. The latter is based on a year of 12 months adding up to 354.37 days. Each lunar month begins at the time of the monthly "conjunction", when the Moon is located on a straight line between the Earth and the Sun. The month is defined as the average duration of a rotation of the Moon around the Earth [29.53 days]. By convention, months of 30 days and 29 days succeed each other, adding up over two years successive months to 59 full days. This leaves only a small monthly variation of 44 mn to account for, which adds up to a total of 24 hours [i.e. the equivalent of one full day] in 2.73 years. To settle accounts, it is sufficient to add one day every three years to the lunar calendar, in the same way that one adds one day to the Gregorian calendar, every four years. The technical details of the adjustment are described in Tabular Islamic Calendar. The Islamic calendar, however, is based on a different set of convictions. Each month has either 29 or 30 days, but usually in no discernible order. Traditionally, the first day of each month is the day [beginnings at sunset] of the first sighting of the hilal [moon] [either because clouds block its view or because the western sky is still too bright when the moon sets...], then the day that begins at that sunset is the 30th. Such a sighting has to be made by one or more trustworthy men testifying before a committee of Muslim leaders. Determining the most likely day that the hilal could be observed was a motivation for Muslim interest in astronomy, which put Islam in the forefront of that science for many centuries. Islamic lunar calendar, consists of twelve months of 29 or 30 days each, is about 11 days shorter than its Georgian equivalent.

Hikam: Aphorisms

Hikmah: Divine wisdom. Literally this means wisdom and refers to the highest possible level of understanding attainable by a Muslim. In particular it refers to the illuminative mystical sort of wisdom which a Gnostic or Sufi might accomplish. Traditional theosophy

Hilal: Crescent moon (month of…)

Hilf al-Fudul: The league of the virtuous

Hima: Wilderness reserve, protected forest, grazing commons, important to khalifa

Himyar: Yemenite kingdom

Hind Bint Utba: The woman who mutilated the body of Muhammad's uncle Hamza at the Battle of Uhud.

Hira: The cave near Mecca where Muhammad received his first revelations Hudaibiyah: a suburb area of Mecca where a treaty was negotiated for the Muslims to return to Mecca after having been forced out

Hiyal: Artifices or tricks, legal methods to circumvent general prohibitions.

Hizb: One half of a juz or roughly 1/60th of the Qur'an party

Hizbollah: Party of God; Shiite militia in southern Lebanon; supported by Iran; anti-Israel.

Holy Land: The term was first used in the Old testament in Zechariah 2:12, see Palestine.

Holy War: See jihad.

Hookah: Terms derived from Arabic and Persian and adopted in India, to designate the apparatus devised for smoking through water. Besides tobacco the mixture might include spices, molasses.

Hoowa: He is

Houri (huriya, pl. huriyat): From the Arabic hur, the plural of hawra an adjective from an Arabic root with the general meaning of whiteness The term is used to describe the beautiful virgins of paradise whose companionship is promised to the believers as part of their eternal reward. They are described in some detail in those passages of the Koran where the joys of heaven are contrasted with the torments of hell. In the Koran the function of the immaculately chaste hours as of the perpetually fresh youths, is to attend and serve the blessed in heaven. Some later commentaries and traditions specify the number of hours and assign them a more explicitly sexual role their virginity being miraculously reconstituted after each encounter. Pleasure mates in Heaven who is soulless and programmed to please our carnal desires.

Hu: The Arabic pronoun, "he", a divine name that refers to the unknown and unnamable Essence of God

Hubal: A god; the chief of the minor deities, was an image of a man, and was said to have been originally brought to Arabia from Syria. Pagan god of the Quraish

Huda: Guidance

Hudaybiyya: A town outside Mecca where a truce was reached between the Quraysh army and the Muslims (was to last 10 years).

Huddud (sing. hadd): Literally limits; the limits of acceptable behavior, the specific punishments designated under sharia for specific crimes, such as intoxication, theft, adultery, and apostasy; legal limits allowed by Islamic Law. Legal penalties and punishments prescribed by Islamic religious law in its strictest interpretation

Hudna: Truce, Cease fire

Hudur: Presence of mind, collectedness, awareness of God's presence

Hujjah: Proof

Hujjaj: Pilgrimage Hukm: Ruling in the Qur'an or Sunnah

Hukm: ruling in the Qur'an or Sunnah. Also spelled **Hukum.**

Hunayn, Valley of: A dry riverbed near Mecca where Muhammad defeated the last large scale resistance to him in Arabia

Hurqalya: The celestial earth, the place of true visions and the Resurrection, the World of Imagination

Huruf muqatta at: Are a group of letters with which several surahs of the Qur'an open. The muqatta at were commonly used by the Arabs at the time of the advent of the Prophet and hence they caused agitation among the Non Muslim audience of that time. This literally style later fell into disuse and hence the commentators of the Quran have come to disagree regarding their exact signification. It is obvious however that deriving guidance from the Qur'an does not depend on grasping the meaning of these letters.

Husinun: Good doers

Husn: Beauty goodness and virtue

Huyay ibn Akhtab: Chief of the exiled Jewish tribe of Nadir.

Father of Safiyya

Hypocrites: Muhammad's opponents

I'dad al 'Oda: Preparation for battle, according to the Quran

I'tikaf: The practice of spiritual retreat by living in the mosque during the last 10 days of Ramadan.

Ibadah: Worship and service to the One God; is used in three meanings: 1) worship and adoration 2) obedience and submission and 3) service and subjection. The fundamental message of Islam is that man as God's creature should direct his ibadah to Him in all the above mentioned meanings and associate none in the rendering of it. Worship, but not limited to ritual, all expressions of servitude to Allah, including the pursuit of knowledge, living a pious life, helping, charity and humility can be considered ibadah.

Iblis: Literally means thoroughly disappointed, one in utter despair. In Islamic terminology it denotes the jinn, who refused the command of God to prostrate before Adam out of Vanity. He also asked God to allow him a term when he might mislead and tempt mankind to error. This term was granted to him by God hereafter he became the chief promoter of evil and prompted Adam and Eve to disobey God's order. He is also called al Shaytan. He is possessed of a specific personality and is not just an abstract force. Satan; also called Shaytan. The Arabic name of the devil no doubt related to the Greek diabolos. He appears in Islamic literature in two roles, one of arrogant disobedience to the commands of God, the other as tempter of Adam and Eve and their descendants. In the latter role, he also commonly called Shaytan, a term clearly related to Satan. According to some versions he is an evil genie more commonly he is regarded in the Islamic as in the Judeo Christian tradition, as a fallen angel. He figures prominently in the Koran and the last chapter. I take refuge with the Lord of mankind, the King of mankind, the God of mankind, from the evil of the insidious tempter who whispers in the hearts of mankind from the genies and from mankind. a creature of the jinn who was banished from the Heavens and cursed until the Last Day for refusing to obey Allah's command. Also known as Satan. A jinn banished to Hell for his arrogance and disobedience, aka Satan: derived from the Greek Diabolos or Devil. He is the equivalent of Lucifer. "Frustrated." The proper name of Satan before he turned to evil.

Ibn Ubbay: Allied himself with a Jewish tribe

Ibn: Son of; used in the Arabic naming system to denote relationships between father and son

Ibrahim: The Islamic name for Abraham.

Ibsan: To do right and to act beautifully, because one knows that Allah is always watching man's actions and thoughts

Id Al-Adha: Ar., the Feast of Sacrifice, commemorating Abraham's sacrifice of a ram as a substitute for his son Isaac, by divine command, the culminating point of the pilgrimage to Mecca. The festival of the sacrifice, on the last day of the Hajj. The festival of Sacrifice, the four day celebration staring on the tenth day of Dhul Hijja The Feast of Sacrifice, in remembrance of Abraham's willingness to obey God and sacrifice his son Ishmael (not

Isaac).

Id Al-Fitr: A holiday, celebrated at the end of Ramadan; "The Breaking of the Fast", on the first day of Shawwal. The festival of breaking the fast at the end of Ramadan. Ar., the celebration of the Breaking of the Fast at the end of fasting in Ramadhan. The festival of Fitr, a religious festival that marks the end of the fast of Ramadan. The celebration of the "Breaking of the Fast", a happy time of feasting and gift-giving.

Id: Festival or Celebration. Sometimes spelled Eid. An Arabic term used to denote the two major religious festivals or holidays of the Islamic year. One of these, the Id al Adha, variously known as the sacrificial Festival or Major Festival is celebrated on the tenth day of the month of Pilgrimage, when the assembled pilgrims make sacrifices in the valley of Mina, in the hills east of Mecca. The practice of sacrificing on this day was not limited to pilgrims, but came to be generally adopted by Sunni Muslims. The second festival the Id al Fitr marked the end of the Fast of Ramadan. It was celebrated on the first day of the following month, Shawwal and sometimes for days after.

Idda: Legally prescribed period during which a woman may not remarry after having been widowed or divorced. Before the finalization of a divorce, the waiting period for a woman to see whether she is pregnant. A waiting period that a woman observes when widowed or divorced before remarrying

'Id ul-Adha: "the Festival of Sacrifice." The four day celebration starting on the tenth day of Dhul-Hijja.

'Id ul-Fitr: "the Festival of Fitr (Breaking the fast)." A religious festival that marks the end of the fast of Ramadan.

I'dad Al-'oda: "preparation for battle" according to Qur'an

Ifriqiyah: North Africa

Iftar: "Evening breakfast" meal; served in the evening during Ramadan. a meal eaten by Muslims breaking their fast after sunset during the month of Ramadan.

Ihada: Act of worship; ritual duty for Muslims; worship and service to the One God.

Ihram: Refers to the state in which the Pilgrim is held to be from the time he performs certain prescribed rituals making his entry into the state of **Ihram** (literally 'prohibiting'). **Ihram** is so called in view of the numerous prohibitions that ought to be observed (e.g. abstention from all sex acts, from the use of perfume, from hunting or killing animals, cutting the beard or shaving the head, cutting the nails, plucking blades of grass or cutting green trees.) A pilgrim's costume, composed only of a white terrycloth, and his state of purity. Ar., the (sacred) dress of a pilgrimage **(haji, q.v.)**, consisting of two lengths of white cotton, one round the waist, the other round the shoulders. denotes the state of consecration which is essentially required for performing Hajj and Umrah. The outward garn which consists in the case of men of just two sheets of cloth instead of tailored clothes is one of the conditions of ihram but not identical with it. Apart from donning that garb one is required to pronounce talbiyah. In the state of ihram the pilgrim is required to observe many prohibitions. He may not hunt, shave or trim hair, shed blood, use perfume or indulge in sexual gratification.

Ihram: Two seamless white garments worn by the pilgrims who make the Hajj, making them all equal.

Ihsan: Compassion, kindness (important Qur'anic concept); literally denotes doing something in a goodly manner. When used in the Islamic religious context, it signifies excellence of behavior arising out of a strong love for God and a profound sense of close relationship with Him. According to a tradition the Prophet defined ihsan as worshipping God as though one sees Him. A desired perfection to comply fully with divine commands; the state of mind of one who strives to be in full compliance with these commands. Perfection in worship, such that Muslims try to worship God as if they see him and although they cannot see him, they undoubtedly believe he is constantly watching over them. The third and most profound level of Muslim spiritual understanding.

Ihtisab: Self-reflection and assessment; observance of religious morality

Ijaz: Miracle, the character of the Quran in both form and content. An elliptical quality of Bedouin speech.

Ijazah: A certificate authorizing one to transmit a subject or text of Islamic knowledge. Certification, diploma.

Ijizas: Biographical dictionary

Ijma (Arabic consensus): One of the four pillars of Islamic jurisprudence ijma means consensus of the community, umma the remaining pillars being the Quran, Prophet Muhammad's sunna later codified as the Hadith and ijtihad interpretative reasoning. Until Muhammad ibn Idris al Shafii founded the discipline of religious jurisprudence based on these pillars ijma had been construed as consensus of ahl al hall wal aqd. But Shafii enlarged it to include the whole community. In more modern times Muhammad Abdu an Egyptian Islamic thinker, interpreted ijma as public opinion. The consensus of the entire Muslim community upon which a legal decision is then delivered. Such judgments could, some twentieth-century Muslim scholars argue, be soundly based on what was deemed best for the community. Collective consensus.

Ijtihad (Arabic: applying effort to form an opinion): Interpretative reasoning with time it became necessary for Muslims and their rulers to interpret the Quran and the Prophet Muhammad's sunna together forming the Islamic law) to address unprecedented situations. By the mid ninth century Ad four major schools of Islamic law ranging between the rigid Hanbali school and the liberal Hanafi school had emerged within Sunni Islam. Unlike in Sunnism in Shia Islam ijtihad did not remain dormant for long the destruction in 1258 of the Sunni Abbasid caliphate by the Mongol ruler Hulagu Khan (1217-65) created a political ideological vacuum in which the Shia doctrine thrived. Jamal al Din ibn Yusuf al Hilli, a shia thinker, rehabilitated the concept and practice of ihtihad. (Arabic reflection): The means by which the early lawyers arrived at legal decisions from the Koran from Tradition or by deduction. In principle all such decisions were consistent, but inevitably they led to the multiplication of local idiosyncrasies and the establishment of the main legal schools replaced individual judgment by generally accepting rules. (Arabic) independent reasoning. During the early times of Islam the possibility of finding a new solution to a juridical problem. Has not been allowed in conservative Islam since the middle ages. However liberal movements within Islam generally argue that any Muslim can perform ijithad given that Islam has no generally accepted clerical hierarchy or bureaucratic organization. Independent judgment on religious matters or principles of Islamic jurisprudence that are not specifically outlined in the Quran. The opposite of ijtihad is taqlid. Arabic for "imitation." The process of personal reflection on the meaning of the Holy Qur'an, allowing individual interpretation of the words and actions of the Prophet Muhammad. Juristic matters.

Ikhlas: Genuine in religious beliefs

Ikhtilaf: Disagreement among the madhhabs (scholars) of a religious principle, opposite of ijma. Juristic differences.

Ikhwan al Safa: Brothers of Purity, a group of Ismail influenced thinkers based in Basra in the tenth century.

Ikraam: Honoring, hospitality, generosity-Dhul jalaali wal ikraam is one of the 99 names of Allah.

Ikrah: mental or physical force.

Ikrimah: Chief of Amir, struggled against Muhaud

Ikrimah: Daughter of Abu Jahl, was the first to accept Islam

Ila: Denotes a husband's vow to abstain from sexual relations with his wife. The maximum permissible limit for abstaining from sexual relations in wedlock under such a vow is four months, after which ila would automatically mean repudiation of the marriage.

Ilah: Deity, a god, including gods worshipped by polytheists.

Ilham: Literally means to suggest to indicate. In Islamic parlance it signifies communicating something directly to a person's heart as a social favor from God rather than as a result of the effort of the person concerned.

Illahi: Divine

Illiyun: The register in which the people of paradise have their names written.

Ilm al-Kalam: Scholastic theology. Islamic theology.

Ilm: Knowledge, but specifically knowledge of God that is collected and systemized. (Arabic) the secret "knowledge" of God, which Shiite Muslims believe to have been the sole possession of the **Imams (q.v.)**; a knowledge of what is right and how Muslims should behave. All varieties of knowledge, usually a synonym for science; knowledge, in particular religious knowledge of ulama.

iltizam: Practice of religion, piety

Imam : Leader of prayer. Imam Abu Hanifah, Imam Malik, Imam ibn Hanbal, Imam al-Shafi'i (A): The four *imams*: Imam Abu Hanifah: Born in al-Kufah A.H. 80 and died in Baghdad A.H. 150. Imam Malik: Born and died in Medina A.H. 94-A.H. 179. Imam Ibn Hanbal: Born and died in Baghdad A.H. 164-A.H. 241. Imam al-Shaf'i: Born in

Askalon, Pakistan A.H. 150 and died in Cairo A.H. 204. These four men systematically developed the rules of conduct and law [*fiqh*] from the injunctions of the Qur'an and the *ahadith*. Four different schools of thought were established after them and each has a slightly different interpretation of the practices of Islam. Imam al-Ghazzali revealed in *Ihya' 'Ulum al-Din* that all four men not only devoted themselves to the knowledge of jurisprudence [*fiqh*] but were also keen observers of the knowledge of the heart (Arabic model one whose leadership or example s to be followed.): religious leader "imam" is used as a noun and as a title. Shias use it for the religious leader at the highest level instead of the honorific caliph used by Sunnis. Thus Shias refer to Ali ibn Abu Talib as Imam Ali, whereas Sunnis call him Caliph Ali. In modern times Ayatollah Ruhollah Khomeini was given this title by Iranian Shias. Finally the leader of prayers at any mosque is called an imam. In the Sunni tradition, a religious leader who leads the prayer; in the Shiite tradition, a descendant of Muhammad who is the divinely chosen leader of the community. Leader at canonical prayer; the one designated to lead the Muslim community for his generation. (Shiites). (1) caliph; (2) prayer leader. Pontiff. A highly respected Muslim leader. Signifies the leader, and in its highest form, refers to the head of the Islamic state. It is also used with reference to the founders of the different systems of theology and law in Islam.

Imamah or imamate: Successorship of Prophet Muhammad and the leadership of mankind.

Imamat: Supreme leadership of Muslims after the Prophet Muhammad Sunnis distinguish between the early caliphate of the Rightly Guided Caliphs, Abu Bakr ibn Abu Qahafa,

Omar ibn Khattab, Othman ibn Affan and Ali ibn Abu Talib and the latter imamat, which was characterized by worldly monarchy. Shias do not accept the imamat of Abu Bakr, Omar, and Othman arguing that the Prophet Muhammad had designated Ali as his successor. The Twelver Shia doctrine formulated by Imam he must be free from sin and error and he must be the most exemplary of all Muslims.

Imami: The school of law adopted by the Twlever Shia. It rejects jihad which can only be proclaimed by the absent imam on his return, and does not recognize the legal dicta of the Umayyad caliphs, but its general attitude is fairly close to the Sunni Hanafis.

Imamis: see Twelver Shias.

Iman: Absolute, complete, and unshakable faith, certitude, and determination that God alone exists; the complete acceptance of the heart that God is One. Also spelled **Eman.** The second level of Muslim spiritual understanding, during which belief is internalized. Belief in God as creator, guide and judge of humankind; belief in God and in Muhammad as His last Prophet. (A) absolute, complete, and unshakable faith, certitude, and determination that God alone exists; the complete acceptance of the heart that God is One. Faith or religious conviction. Faith, belief, a central organizing principle of Islam. Faith, submission to God through the heart.

Iman Islam: The state of the spotlessly pure heart which contains Allah's Holy Qur'an, His divine radiance, His divine wisdom, His truth, His prophets, His angels, and His laws. When the resplendence of Allah is seen as the completeness within this pure heart of man that is *Iman-Islam*. When the complete, unshakable faith of this pure heart is directed toward the One who is completeness and is made to merge with that One; when that heart trusts only in Him and worships only Him, accepting Him as the only perfection and the only One worthy of worship – that is *Iman-Islam*

Imja: The consensus of religious scholars on points of Islamic law.

In sha Allah: Literally if God pleases, the Islamic equivalent of please God, deo volente, and the like. Among Muslims, this is used much more extensively than among Jews or Christians at the present time. To omit it in any statement about the future is regarded as an impiety, even as a provocation. It is sometimes also used with statements about the past, usually to express doubt. An interesting example is provided in a report, preserved in the archives of the Republic of Venice, and sent by its diplomatic envoy in the Ottoman capital, Istanbul. Dated October 1588, the report contains the following passage: "Today the English envoy went to the Pashas and told them that the Spanish armada had been defeated. They said: In Sha Allah, which means the astute Venetian diplomat added "that they didn't believe him."

Incarnation: The embodiment of God in human form.

Indigenous: Originating in a place rather than arriving from another place.

Infanticide: Killing of a newborn, especially female.

Infaq: The habitual inclination to give rather than take in life, the basis for charity.

Infidel: Any who do not accept the religious faith of the person speaking; one who rejects the teachings of Islam; one who lacks thankfulness; un-believer.

Inimitability: The quality of something that makes it matchless.

Injil: The Arabic name for the Gospel or **Evangel** of Jesus. The revelations of Jesus. Arabic term for the holy book called The Gospel said to have been given to Jesus, who is known as Isa in Arabic, Muslims believe the holy book has been lost and the New Testament gospels (Matthew, Mark, Luke and John) are not the word of Allah only Christian stories about Jesus. Signifies the inspired rations and utterances of Jesus which he delivered during the last two or three years of his earthly life in his capacity as a Prophet. The Injil mentioned by the Quran should however not be identified by the four Gospels of the New Testament which contain a great deal of material in addition to the inspired statements of the Prophet material in addition to the inspired statements of the Prophet Jesus. Presumably the statements explicitly attributed to Jesus In the Gospels contain substantively the same teachings as those of the Quran.

Innaa Lillaahi Wa Innaa Ilayhi Raaji'oon: To Allah we belong to Him is our return, said to mourners.

Insaf: Justice

Insan: True man; a true human being; the true form of man; the form of Allah's qualities, actions, conduct, behavior, and virtues. One who has the completeness of this form and has filled himself with these qualities is an *insane*. Human being, from the root meaning to be companionable, agreeable or genial.

Insan Kamil: Perfect man, God-realizing being. One who has realized Allah as his only wealth, cutting away all the wealth of the world. The perfect person; used for the Prophet

Insha Allah: If it is God's (Allah's) will; "If it pleases Allah"; "God willing."

Intifada: (Arabic: shivering or shaking off). Palestinian uprising against the Israeli occupation 1987-93. Intifada erupted spontaneously in the Palestinian refugee camp of Jabaliya In the Gaza Strip on 9 December 1987, when thousands marched in protest against the killing of four Palestinians by an Israeli truck near the settlement. *The intifada stemmed from twenty years of collective and individual frustration and humiliation that the Palestinians had endured in their dealings with the Jews and the Israeli authorities, both military and civilian. By early January 1988 the secular PLO had set up the United National Leadership of the Uprising to direct the movement while the Islamic center formed Hamas for the same purpose. The campaign against the Israeli agents intensified in the early 1990s and destroyed Shin Beth's 20,000 strong intelligence network among the Palestinians, making it extremely hard for the occupying Israeli authorities to reimpose full control and restore law and order. By the end of the intifada 1,636 Palestinians including 316 minors had been killed 1,346 by the Israeli security forces and 290 by Jewish civilians.

Iqamah: The second call to prayer. Similar to the azhan.

Iqra: Recite: Gabriel ordered Muhammad. Read the first word of revelation given to Muhammad and the origin of the word Quran Read.

Iqta: Non hereditary grant of land by a ruler to a soldier or an administrative official in lieu of pay, conditional upon further service. It was particularly developed by the Great Seljuks who had adopted the Sasanian view of the ruler as sole proprietor of his domains, though even in Mamluk Egypt no more than half the land was made iqta. It is somewhat comparable to medieval European fiefs, but the comparison must not be strained.

Irfan: The Muslim mystical tradition. Gnostic. Knowledge

Irhab: Terror or terrorism

irhan: Terror or terrorism

Irtidad: Apostasy, see murtadd. Also Riddah.

Isa: Jesus "Isa ibn Maryam (English, Jesus son of Mary), a matronymic (since he had no biological father. The Quran asserts that Allah has no sons and therefore "Isa is not the son of Allah. Muslims honor Isa as a nabi and rasoul.

Isbraq: (Arabic) illumination. The Ishraqi school of philosophy and spirituality was founded by Yahya Suhrawardi.

Isha': (Night) Prayer signifies the prescribed Prayer which is performed after the night has well set in. Night, prayer signifies one of the five prayers which is performed after the night has set in and the red glow of sunset has disappeared

Isharat: Hints, indications

Ishmael: Son of Abraham and Hagar.

Ishq: Love, transformative love for God.

Ishraq: Illumination, the school of philosophy established by Suhraqardi

Ishraqiyyun: Followers of Ishraq

Islam and Muslims: (Arabic: submission to God's will): "Surrendering to God and attaining peace." The Arabic name for the religion taught by Muhammad. The last of the three important monotheistic religions, which draws upon Judaism and Christianity, Islam was founded by the Prophet Muhammad, who was born in Mecca those who follow Islam are called Muslims. Next in importance to Muslims is the sunna (custom) the words and deeds of the Prophet Muhammad. The Quran and the Sunna, later codified as the Hadith together from the Sharia Islamic law, which covers all aspects of religious, social and political life, including state administration and conduct of war. After the death of the Prophet Muhammad, who during the last decade of his life governed a domain fought wars and acted as a judge and administrator, his duties were taken over by his vice regent, Caliph Abu Bakr ibn Abu Quhafa. He was followed by Omar ibn Khattab, and Othman ibn Affan who was assassinated by Muhammad ibn Abu Bakr and other conspirators for his maladministration. The rule of Caliph Ali ibn Abu Talib (AD 656-61), a cousin and son in law of the Prophet Muhammad were challenged by Muwaiya ibn Abu Sufiyan, governor of Syria. A mystical streak within Islam known as Sufism was developed among others by Abu Hamid Muhammad al Ghazali (1058-1111). The spread of Islam was rapid during the two centuries after the Prophet Muhammad's death reaching central France in 732 AD. In 2002, there were over 1.6 billion adherents of Islam worldwide Surrender to God; the last religion of God delivered to the last Prophet through the revelation of the Quran. Surrender and commitment

Islamdom: The lands where Muslim communities are present.

Islamic banking: The Quran forbids usury: " Oh believers fear you God and give up the usury that is outstanding if you are believers 2:279 and Oh believers devour not usury doubled and redoubled and fear you God. 3:25. Money must be used only as a means of exchange. The circumventing devices are muraabaha, mudaaraba and mushaaraka. Muraabaha involves selling a commodity with a contract that it would be bought back later at a premium equaling the agreed interest.

Islamic Calendar: In Islam, as in Judaism, a day starts with sunset. The Islamic calendar is dated from the sunset on 15 July AD 622, the start of the hijra of the Prophet Muhammad from Mecca to Medina. The Islamic year is lunar and contains 354 days 8 hours and 4.8 minutes. A person aged 100 by a solar calendar is 103 according to a lunar calendar. To convert an Islamic date to a Christian date, divide it by 1.031 and then add 621 or 622 depending on the month of the year.

Islamic dress: Islamic dress applies to women who are required to behave as stated in the Qur'anic verse "and say to the believing women that they cast their eyes and guard their private parts and let them cast their veils over their bosoms.

The intention is to avoid arousing sexual passion between men and women who are not spouses or are not intending to be. Islamic dress has been compulsory for women in Saudi Arabia ever since its founding in 1932. Following the Islamic revolution in Iran in 1979, it was made compulsory by law. Iran's urban working class and rural women wear a chador an all encompassing shroud.

Islamic fundamentalism: Fundamentalism is the term used for the effort to define the fundamentals of a religion and adhere to them. Whether a Muslim majority state today is fundamentalist or not can be judged by a single criterion: It is legislation derived solely from the Sharia. By this standard Saudi Arabia is the oldest Islamic fundamentalist state in the world. Since its inception in 1932, it has known nothing but the Sharia. The belief that the revitalization of Islamic society can only come about through a return to the fundamental principles and practices of early Islam. Fundamentalist movements have often been a response to political and economic decline, which is ascribed to spiritual and moral decay. These movements shared the belief that religion is integral to both state and society and advocated a return to a life patterned on the 7th century political community of the faithful established by Muhammad at medina, governed by the Shari (Islamic law), and supported if need be by Jihad (holy war). No doubt that the Iranian revolution has been an inspiring example to many Muslims of all persuasions throughout the world.

Islamic law: *see* Sharia

Islamic: Pertaining to the civilization of Islam.

Islamicate: Pertaining to the civilization of Islam.

Islamism and Islamists: When Islam is used as a political ideology, it is described as Islamism and its adherents are called Islamists. The ideological belief in the requirement to enact the political tenets of Islam as the basis of political life.

Ism, The personal name: The most popular names all over the Muslim world are still the Arab names sanctified by scripture and early Muslim history. They may be of several types, of which the following are the most common: a) Biblical names in their Koranic forms, such as Harun (Aaron), Ibrahim (Abraham), Sulayman (Solomon) and Ismail (Ishmael). B)..Other Arab names, largely pre Islamic in origin, most of them being Arabic adjectives or nouns, e.g. Ahmad, Ali, Hasan, Husain, Muhammad, Uthman. Some of these are often used with the Arabic definite article. C) Compound named, usually consisting of Abd (slave) followed by Allah or by one of the ninety nine divine attributes such as Abd al Aziz, slave of the mighty, Abd al Majid Slave of the glorious, Abd al Karim slave of the generous. Other compounds with Allah are also used: nimat Allah grace of God, Hibat Allah Gift of God.

Isma: Impeccability (of Shia imam)

Isma'ili: The name of a sub sect of the Shi'a.

Ismail: The prophet who is known as Ishmael in the Bible, the eldest son of Abraham, who was cast out into the wilderness at God's command with his mother, Hagar, but saved by God. Muslim tradition has it that Hagar and Ismail in Mecca that Abraham came to visit them there and that Abraham and Ismail rebuilt the Kabah (which had been originally constructed by Adam, the first prophet and father of mankind).

Ismaili: A branch of Shiite Islam that recognizes seven rather than 12 *imams* (spiritual leaders). They include Mustalians in India and Yemen, and Nizaris in Afghanistan, East Africa, India, Iran, and Syria. Ismail, the eldest son of the sixth *imam*, Jafar al-Sadia (d. 765) was disinherited and most Shiites recognized his brother Musa al-Kazim as *imam*. Ismailis regarded Ismail as the seventh and last *imam* and expected that he would soon return as the Mahdi (expected one) to overthrow existing corrupt governments and establish justice on earth. The Fatimid dynasty (909-1171) promoted their beliefs in Egypt and Syria but attempted no mass conversions among the Sunni majority. The Ismailis developed the idea that the religious precepts have a secret inner meaning, passed from Muhammad to Ali and from him to later imams, who could thus instruct the ignorant. A group of Shias recognizing Ismail., the son of the sixth imam Jafar al Sadiq as their Messiah. In the late 9th century they appear as a missionary movement radiating from Iraq to Khurasan and Transoxania, Bahrein, the Maghrib, Yemen and Sind, though the advent of the Ismaili Fatimids caused internal dissensions which were accentuated by extremists like the Assassins in Persia and Syria, and the different communities tended to draw apart. Communities of Ismailis survived the Mongols, particularly in Transoxania, but the most important group today are the adherents of the Agha Khan. Islamic group Part of Shia Islam, Ismailies are distinguished from the other sub sects Zaidis and Imamis or twelvers by the number of revered figured they regard as Imams. An Ismaili group set up the Fatimid. Muhammad and the wife of Imam Ali, caliphate in

Tunis which after conquering Egypt also in AD 969 rivaled the Abbasids, based on Baghdad their rule lasted until 1171.

Isnad: Support, chain of authorities transmitting a hadith thus guaranteeing its validity. A chain of narration.

Isra: Miracle, such as the Night Journey.

Isra: Muhammad's miraculous journey from Mecca to Jerusalem on the winged Buraq. support, chain of authorities transmitting a hadith thus guaranteeing its validity. Prophet Muhammad's journey to the Heavens and back. The Night Journey of the Prophet Muhammad to Jerusalem and back to Mecca.

Israfil: The angel who will blow the trumpet, signaling Judgment Day.

Istigfar: Requesting forgiveness

Istihada: Vaginal bleeding except Haid and Nifas.

Istihsan: Personal welfare

Istihsan and istislah: General principles of equity used by the Muslims schools of law to supplement legal reasoning by analogy, generally as a justification for revisions of practice in the light of changed circumstances. Istihsan, favored by Hanafis, is a particular interpretation of the law by a judge's own deliberation.

Istikhabarat: Intelligence

Istish'had: Martyrdom.

Istislah: Public interest-a source of Islamic Law. Collective welfare.

Itaqu: The faithful who fear Allah.

Itazahu: Withdrew

Ithim: Negative reward for bad deeds that is tallied on qiyamah (Judgment Day.) Opposite of thawab.

Ithm: Denotes negligence, dereliction of duty and sin. For details see **Surah** 7, n. 25.

Ithna Ashari: Twelve Imam Shiism; resting on the belief in the twelve Imams; dominant in Iran.

Itikaf: Refers to the religious practice of spending the last ten days of Ramadan in a mosque so as to devote oneself exclusively to worship. In this state one may go out of the mosque only for the absolutely necessary requirements of life. But one must stay away from gratifying one's sexual desire. seclusion in the masjid for the purpose of worship usually performed during the last ten days of Ramadan.

Itizal: Parting company

Itizam: Tax-farming or tax-gathering concession

Itmam al Hujjah: Clarification of truth in its ultimate form.

Ittihad **(A):** Unity

Iwan: Open porch, normally with a pointed barrel vault and fronting a domed chamber, either a throne room or the mihrab of a great mosque. Iwans were an important element of Sasanian palace architecture but their origins appear to be Mesopotamian, notably Assur/Ashur in the Parthian period.

Izzah: Denotes a position which is at once exalted and secure. In other words, the term signifies inviolable honor and glory.

Ja'afari: A branch of Sha'ariah, Islamic law, followed mainly by Shias

Jaa'iz: That which is allowed or permissible. As a rule, everything that is not prohibited is allowed. (see halal, mustahabb, mandub)

Jaafari Code: Shia Islamic legal school, This Islamic legal code is named after Imam Jaafar al Sadiq (AD 699-765), the sixth Imam of Twelver Shias.

Jabal un Nur: Mountains of Light

Jabarut: "Mightiness, the intelligible, spiritual world, commonly contrasted with malakut and mulk.

Jabl un-Nur: Mountain of Light

Jadhba: Attraction, the divine power that draws people to God, contrasted with suluk

Jafari: Referring to the sole Shi'ite madhhab ascribed to the Imam Ja'far al Sadiq

Jahaliyyah: "Ignorance." Refers to the time before the advent of Islam when superstitious and barbaric customs were a part of Arabian life.

Jahangir: A Mughal ruler

Jahannam: Hell, where people are punished in the hereafter; for the wrongdoers.

Jahannam: The hell fire, hell; the punishment of Hell

Jahannum: The hell fire, hell; the punishment of Hell; from Gehenna: a place of torment and punishment in the afterlife. In the Koran, it sometimes appears as a synonym of hell or hellfire. The more usual term is Nar, literally fire. In the Islamic perception, hell is made up of a descending sequence of layers. The upper levels are reserved for unrepentant Muslim sinners, the lower for infidels. The torments of hell are described in some detail in the Koran and in later Islamic writings

Jahili: Ignorant; the state of the world before Islam.

Jahiliyah: The state of ignorance prevailing in Arabia before Islam; denotes all those world-views and ways of life which are based on rejection or disregard of heavenly guidance communicated to mankind through the Prophets and Messengers of God; the attitude of treating human life – either wholly or partly – as independent of the directives of God.

Jahl: Ignorance, hence jahiliya period of ignorance or pre Islamic times.

Jaish: army

Jallam ibn Mishkan: Chief of Jewish tribe Bani Nadir (Kia'b's tribe).

Jalsa: Sitting

Jamaa: association, group, company

Jamaat: Group or society; congregation.

Jami: The great mosque in which alone the khutba might be said on Fridays. The early sources use the term minbar and even great mosques like that of Ibn Tulun in Cairo are described as masjids. The first occurrence of jami in an inscription is in Fatimid Egypt. Thereafter the term gained acceptance.

Jami': The congregations mosque used particularly, though not only, on Fridays for the weekly sermon and noon prayer

Jami'ah: Gathering, i.e. a university, a mosque or more generally a community or association.

Jamiat: Association

Jan: Persian for soul, spirit, life

Janabah: A ceremonial impurity that necessitates full ghusl ablution; the state of major ritual impurity which is caused by menses, coitus, child birth or pollutes nocturnal. In the state of janabah one may not perform the prayers.

Janabat: An unclean state of body caused by discharge of semen or sexual intercourse

Janazah: Funeral rites in Islam.

Jannah: Garden of Eden; Paradise., Heaven.

Jash: Literally, 'little donkeys'; derisory term used about Kurdish

117

tribal irregulars employed by Iraqi government, the National Defense Battalions

Jayilihha (adjective, jahili): The Age of Ignorance. Originally the term was used to describe the pre-Islamic period in Arabia. Today Muslim fundamentalists often apply it to any society, even a nominally Muslim society, which has, in their view, turned its back upon God and refused to submit to God's sovereignty.

Jaysh: Army

Jazakallahu Khayran: "May God reward you for the good. Islamic expression of gratitude.

Jebel ul-Tarik: Mountain of Tarik

Jesus in Islam: (Arabic: *'Isa*) Is a messenger of God who had been sent to guide the Children of Israel (*bani isra'il*) with a new scripture, the *Injil* (gospel). The Qur'an, believed by Muslims to be God's final revelation, states that Jesus was born to Mary (Arabic: Maryam) as the result of virginal conception, a miraculous event which occurred by the decree of God (Arabic: Allah). To aid him in his quest, Jesus was given the ability to perform miracles, all by the permission of God. According to Islamic texts, Jesus was neither killed nor crucified, but rather he was raised alive up to heaven. Islamic traditions narrate that he will return to earth near the day of judgment to restore justice and defeat *al-Masih ad-Dajjal* (lit. "the false messiah", also known as the Antichrist). Like all prophets in Islam, Jesus is considered to have been a Muslim as he preached for people to adopt the straight line path in submission to God's will. Islam rejects that Jesus was God incarnate or the son of God, stating that he was an ordinary man who, like other prophets, had been divinely chosen to spread God's message. Islamic texts forbid the association of partners with God (*shirk*), emphasizing the notion of God's divine oneness (*tawhid*). Numerous titles ("the messiah: the anointed one" i.e. by means of blessings), although it does not correspond with the meaning accrued in Christian belief. Jesus is seen in Islam as a precursor to Muhammad, and is believed by Muslims to have foretold the latter's coming.

Jews in Arab Middle East: In 1945 there were 870,000 Jews in the Arab Middle East.. Following the founding of Israel and the First Arab Israeli War their number fell to 70,000 with 600,000 migrating to Israel and the rest elsewhere.

Jibrail: The angel Gabriel.

Jibt: Signifies a thing devoid of any true basis and bereft of usefulness. In Islamic terminology the various forms of sorcery, divination and soothsaying, in short all superstition are called jibt

Jihad: Holy war. The greater **jihad** or religious war is waged by the believer against his evil desires and bad qualities. The external **jihad**, prescribed by the **shari'ah** for the repulsion of oppressors, must be conducted under a truly righteous **imam** within rigid restrictions and may be continued only to the limit of what is needed to repel the aggressors. (Arabic: effort): Full title in Arabic: Jihad fi sabil Allah (Striving in the way of God). Literally, jihad means effort of struggle, which is waged in various forms-internal and external-and degrees, war being the most extreme. Historically the term jihad had been used to describe an

119

armed struggle by Muslims against unbelievers in their mission to advance Islam or counter danger to it. According to the sunna, jihad is to be launched only after unbelievers have rejected the offer to Muslims or dhimmis. 'struggle in the way of God'. In the Koran, this probably refers to the early Muslim razzias against pagan opponents, particularly the Meccans. Later, any war undertaken in the name of Islam against unbelievers or backsliders. Sometimes used in a non-military, quasi-metaphorical sense. (C.F. 'crusade'.) war against unbelievers according to the *Shari'a*. Struggle; can be any struggle, from a personal striving to fulfill religious responsibilities to a holy war undertaken for the defense of Islam. Inner struggle against the unwholesome part of one's nature; struggle against oppression and the enemies of Islam.

Jihād al Saghir: Offensive jihad declared by caliph.

Jihād al talab: Offensive jihad.

Jihād al daf'a: Defensive jihad.

Jihād bil mal: Financial jihad.

Jihād bis saif: literally 'struggle by the sword'; holy war.

Jihad-I-Akbar: The greater struggle

jihadi: Supporter of jihad

Jilbab: a long, flowing, baggy garment worn by some to fulfill the mandates of sartorial hijab. Some more conservative Muslims believe that jilbab is incumbent upon Muslim women to wear this as a sign of modesty. (See Abaya,

Burka, and Chador.) The over garment worn by Muslim women

Jilbab: Islamic outer garment; worn outside house.

Jim'ah : The traditional gathering for prayers on Friday

Jima: Consensus

Jinn: An angel created from fire; has free will to obey or disobey Allah.

Jinn: An independent species of creation about which little is known except that unlike man, who was created out of earth, the **jinn** were created out of fire. But like man, a Divine Message has also been addressed to them and they too have been endowed with the capacity, again like man, to choose between good and evil, between obedience or disobedience to God. Ambivalent spirits that inhabit an intermediate world between the known or material world and the unknown or spiritual world; the English counterpart is genie. "Hidden ones." The term used for a class of invisible spirits that inhabits another dimension. They can communicate with us only through our minds. There are good and evil jinn. The caricature of the genie is based on this creature.

Jinns: Spirits with bodies of vapor or flame.

Jizya Tax: The term in the technical language of Shari'a, for the poll tax payable by tolerated non Muslims under Muslim rule. The term already appears in the Koran: "Fight against those who do not believe in God or in the last day and do not forbid what God and his Prophet have forbidden and do not follow the true faith, until they pay the jizya from the hand and humbly. Its payment continues to be an essential part of the status of Dhimmi. The methods of assessment and collection varied from time to time and from place to place. By the 19th century, the idea of a poll tax on people of another faith was no longer acceptable to enlighten modern opinion. There was however a temporary solution. Another aspect of the dhimma was a ban on bearing arms and the poll tax could thus be conveniently replaced by a military service exemption tax. At the present time both the ban and poll tax have been relinquished; tribute. In an Islamic state, all Muslims have the duty to protect the community from outside aggression, including the duty to bear arms if necessary. In addition, wealthy Muslims are required in the faith to pay alms (zakat). Minority religious communities enjoy the protection of the Islamic state, but are exempt from these requirements. The Islamic state imposes a tax (called *jizyah*) on non-Muslims within its borders, to fund the army and ensure their continued protection. The word "jizyah" itself means to "compensate" or "repay." The non-Muslims who enjoy the freedoms of living in the Islamic state need to compensate for their exemption from military duty and the payment of alms. Those who are old, sick, or unable to pay are exempt from the jizyah. Unbelievers are required to pay **jizyah** (poll tax) in lieu of security provided to them as the **Dhimmis** (Protected People) of an Islamic state, and their exemption from military service and payment of **Zakah**. **Jizyah** symbolizes the submission of the unbelievers to the suzerainty of Islam.

Johad: (lit)effort; (fig) Holy war

Judgment Day: Judgment day or Doomsday, central point of early

Christian, Jewish, and Islamic eschatology, sometimes called the Day of the Lord. References to it throughout the Bible are numerous. The Christian belief in the Last Judgment asserts that this world will end, the dead will be raised up in the general resurrection, and God, or his agent, will gloriously come to judge the living and the dead. The sinners shall be cast into hell, and the righteous shall live in heaven. These concepts are also common themes in early Jewish apocalyptic speculation. Doomsday believers are called chiliasts, millenarians, or, specifically, Adventists.

Juhud: Too deny, Jaahid (the denier). Disbelief out of rejection. When there comes to them that which they should have recognized, they refuse to believe in (kafaru) it. (2:89) Accordingly, juhud includes rejection (Kufr at Taktheeb) and resistance. (kufr al inaad.)

Juma: *Juma* means Friday in Arabic; the *juma* congregational prayers, which occur on Fridays, are the most important prayers of the week for Muslims

Jumu'ah: The gathering, the prayer that Muslim men must attend on Friday afternoon

Jund Allah: The army of God

Junub: An unclean state of body as in breaking Wudu

Juz: One of thirty parts of the Quran. (A) portion; section.

Ka'abah: A shrine located in the center of Mecca; cube-shaped building; contained a black stone (meteorite) and some 300 other gods and goddesses (removed and destroyed by Muhammad). The temple of Allah, the High God of the

Arab. A temple in Mecca that, according to Islamic tradition, was built by Adam and rebuilt by the prophet Abraham and his son Ishmael. Qa'aba, originally dedicated to Allah.

Ka'b bin Al Ashraf: A Jewish poet in Mecca who mocked Muhammad in his verses and was assassinated on Muhammad's orders. a Jewish poet of the Bani Nadir Tribe. Muhammad had him assassinated.

Ka'b ibn Asad: Chief of Qurayzah

Ka'b ibn Asad: Chief of the Jewish tribe Banu Qurayzah.

Ka'bah: Cubic building in Makka containing the Black Stone, believed by Muslims to be a fragment of the original temple of Abraham. Focus of Prayer and the hajj. See also Qibla. Originally a cubic construction covered with a black veil housing a Black Stone, associated in Islam with a Sanctuary, built by Abraham at Mecca though it was evidently the center of a pre Islamic cult of idols in the form of stones. Sometimes known as the house of God, bayt Allah a cube like building situated in the center of the Great Mosque in Mecca. It is the central and most respected sanctuary of Islam. The door of the façade, facing northeast, is about two meters above ground level and can be reached by wooden steps on wheels. The black stone is in the eastern corner. Muslims all over the world pray in the direction of the Ka'ba, and every year, pilgrims make it the focal point of their pilgrimage. According to the Koran, the foundations of the Ka'ba were laid by Abraham and his son Ishmail. the Holy House, or shrine of Islam, in the Grand Mosque at Mecca. In Islam, the *Ka'bah* is the most important for worship. The place where the earlier prophets

124

and the Final Prophet, Muhammad, gathered together in prayer. On the part of *shari'ah*, one of the five obligations, or *furud*, is the pilgrimage to the *Kab'ah* known as *hajj*. Another meaning: the innermost heart, or *qalb*, when is the original source of prayer; the place where a true man, or *insane*, meets Allah face to face. Whoever brings his heart to that state of perfection and prays to God from that heart will be praying from the *Kab'ah*

Kaffarah: Means atonement, expiation.

Kafir (pl. Kafiroon): He who rejects God. Non-believer. Signifies one who denies or rejects the truth, i.e. who disbelieves in the message of the Prophets. Since the advent of Muhammad (peace be on him), anyone who rejects his Message is a **kafir**. An Arabic word meaning unbeliever from a verb meaning to disbelieve or deny. The Turkish form is gavur. It is the term commonly used in Arabic and other Islamic languages to denote non Muslims. Islamic law and practice make an important distinction between two categories of unbelievers: The first form is gavur. It is the term commonly used in Arabic and other Islamic languages to denote non Muslims. Islamic law and practice make an important distinction between two categories of unbelievers: The first consists of monotheists to whom at some time in the past God sent prophets who brought books of revelation. In principle, this category consisted of Jews, Christians, and a third group known as the Sabaens or Sabi'a. For many centuries now, it has been limited to Jews and Christians and the books in Question to the Old and New Testaments. These when they come under the authority of the Muslims state, may be accorded the status of dhimmi. The second category are those who have no book or at least none recognized by Islam as a divine origin and who worship false or plural Gods. These according to the holy law, may not be accorded tolerance, but must be given choice of conversion or death. The latter may, however be commuted to enslavement. Some have suggested that the term kafir should apply only to the second and not the first category.

Kahin: Traditional shamanistic soothsayer in Arabia at the time of Muhammad.

Kahins: The soothsayers of Arabia

Kahinum: A priestly tribe in Arabia

Kalam Allah: Word of God

Kalam: (Arabic) literally, "debates." Muslim theology: the attempt to interpret the Koran in a rational way; a discussion, based on Islamic assumptions, of theological questions. The term is often used to describe the tradition of Muslim scholastic theology. Debate on matters of Muslim theology and cosmology. *See also* Ahl al Kalam. Literally "words or speech" and referring to oration. The name applied to the discipline of philosophy and theology concerned specifically with the nature of faith, determinism and freedom, and the nature of the divine attributes. Muslims scholastic theology, devoted to solving problems raised by Koranic interpretation the ascription of anthropomorphic predicates to God the freedom of the will. By rational argument and not dogmatic pronouncement.

Kalam: Talk; theology

Kalimah: Affirmation of faith. *La ilah illa Allah*: There is nothing other than You, O God. Only You are Allah. The recitation or remembrance of God which cuts away the influence of the five elements (earth, fire, water, air, and ether), washes away all the karma that has accumulated from the very beginning until now, dispels the darkness, beautifies the heart and causes it to resplend The *kalimah* washes the body and the heart of man and makes them pure, makes his wisdom emerge, and impels that wisdom to know the self and God. Lit.: the word. See also: *dhikr, la ilah illa Allah*

Kalipha: Khalifa

Kanuni: Law giver

Kashf: Unveiling of the ultimate reality (Sufism)

Katib: Writer, specifically secretary in government office.

Kaza: District

Kazi Mullah: Dervish

Keemahs: Head-covering.

Khaifati-Rasulil Lah: A successor to the Messenger of God.

Khaijites: One of them killed Ali, as he was entering a mosque at Kura, Iraq

Khair: Every kind of good

Khala: Auntie

Khalifah: "Caretaker." The term for the supreme leader of the Muslim community after the passing of the Prophet.

Spelled as **caliph** in English. Caliph, the deputy of God on earth. In Qur'an applied to Adam, and hence to all humanity in relation to the rest of creation; specifically applied to the early successors of the Prophet as leaders of the Islamic state or khilafa and to the successors of founders of Islamic states or Sufi tariqas. Caliph, the one who comes after the Prophet, the titular leader of Muslims until the caliphate was abolished in 1924. Caliph, a deputy, or successor, took position of the umma leadership following Muhammad's death in 632 ACE. Caretaker, replacement. Replacement; Muslim leader of the umma after Muhammad's death.

Khalifat Rashidun: Four first caliphs, believed by most Muslims to be most righteous rulers in history

Khalifat Rasul Allah: Successor of the messenger of God. A caliph.

Khalil: Devoted friend.

Khaliq: Creator, Allah

Khaliqa: Creation

Khalq: Creation, the act of measuring; determining, estimating and calculating. Khalq is the noun form of the verb khalaqa (see bara, sawwara); people.

khalwa: Proximity between two unmarried people

Khalwat dar anjuman: retreat within society, living in the presence of God while participating actively in the community. withdrawal from society to focus on spiritual exercises and inner purification

Khamar: (Khamr) Intoxicant, wine. An intoxicating Arabian drink, forbidden in Islam. literally means wine and has been prohibited by Islam. This prohibition covers everything that acts as an agent of intoxication.

Khamsin: An Arabic word meaning 50. The name of a hot windstorm from the south or southeast that blows periodically in the spring.

Khan: (i) a hostelry for merchants; (ii) a ruler, correctly **khaqan,** a Turkish title with no relation to (i). A Turko Mongol princely title probably a contradiction of khaqan. In both forms, the title occurs at an early date but its best known through its adoption by the great Mongol conqueror Jengiz and his successors. It was also used by others exercising sovereign authority, among them the Ottoman sultans. Like other titles, it underwent a process of gradual devaluation. Among the Turks and Arabs, it has disappeared; in Iran and Central Asia, it survived rather longer as an equivalent of mister. It sometimes appears as a family name. Khan is also used to designate a large building for the accommodation of travelers and their wares. In this sense it is the equivalent of caravanserai. Caravansary, both urban and rural providing loading and some protection for merchants, quarters for government officials and accommodation for trade. Some rural khans are known to have been pious foundation those in towns were generally not and were a convenient way for local notables to tap the gains from international trade

Khanaqah: A Sufi center. Convent

Khanqah: Sufi hospice mainly in areas of Persian influence; a building where such Sufi **(q.v.)** activities as dhikr **(q.v.)** take place, where Sufi masters live and instruct their disciples. An endowed foundation governed by a shakh with provision for the maintenance of Sufis/ Khanqahs were particularly popular as funerary foundation in 12th and 13th century Syria and 13th to 15th century Egypt. They are in some respects similar to medieval Europeans monasteries except that there was no specific rule to govern the order. Often however they were so richly endowed that their inmate must have found even spiritual poverty difficult to practice.

Khanum: A feminine form of the Turko Mongol Khan. Like its masculine equivalent, it has gradually declined from a princely title to a polite form of address for ladies.

Kharaj: A land tax

Kharijis: Seceders. Secessionists. The party refused to recognize Ali's treaty with his opponents after his death at Siffin with the result that in their view any miscreant imam loses his divine authority becoming an infidel and may be removed it necessary by force. (adj. or noun): the branch of Islam that developed in the seventh century from the conviction that the most capable Muslim should become caliph; outsider or succeeder

Kharijite: Polemical name applied to a member of certain extremists Islamist groups that condemn all other Muslims as sinners; early Muslim sectaries who believed in a wholly elective Caliphate, and rejected the doctrine of justification without works. Succeeders, killers of Ali (661).

Kharja: Envoy

Khatib: the speaker at the Friday Muslim prayer or Jumu'ah prayer.

Khatm al-Anbiya: Seal of the Prophets (Muhammad)

Khatm: Complete recitation of the Quran. Seal or stamp, referring to the fact that Muhammad is the last of the prophets.

Khatmi Qur'an: The name of the ceremony celebrating a child's first completion of reading the entire Qur'an. Also called an **ameen** ceremony.

Khattab ibn Nufayl: One of Muhammad's most trusted companions.

Khawaja: In Egyptian dialect, Khawaga. At one time widely used in the Arabic speaking countries as a polite form of address for foreigners, specifically non-Arab, non Muslim foreigners. The word is derived from the Persian Khaja, a term used as a specially respectful form of address to a rich merchant, a senior scholar or teacher, a venerable old man, a lord or master, a vizier or other high dignitary of state. It is also used perhaps ironically to address a eunuch. The Turkish form hoca pronounced hodja is used to address or refer to a Muslim man of religion or in a secular context to a teacher. A famous example Is the Hodja Nasreddin Efendi, hero of a rich folklore of humorous anecdotes.

Khawarij: Rebels of Islam. Fundamentalists that emerged from the ranks of Ali's supporters, espoused dictatorship of the seemingly virtuous – they declared both Uthman and Ali as un-Islamic traitors and un-believers. Known for their extreme pietism while preparing rebellion and mass murder. Many of their leaders came from the Banu Tamin, a powerful Najd tribe of which Ibn Abd al-Wahhab, more than 1,000 years later, was a member. Dissenders (order of...)

Khayal: Imagination, image; the intermediate realm of the soul, between spirit and body

Khaybar: Jewish Oasis in Medina. An oasis near Medina which Muhammad attacked, exiling the Jews who inhabited it Jewish settlement, Muhammad's enemy. Destroyed by Muhammad.

Khayr: That which is right or good; that which is acceptable to wisdom and to Allah, as opposed to *sharr*, that which is evil or bad; goodness, see Birr (righteousness). See Qist (Equity), see Adl (equilibrium and justice), see Haqq (truth and right) See Ma'ruf (known and approved) See Taqwa (piety.)

Khazir: see Khizr

Khazraj: A tribe in Mecca

Khedive: A division of the Ismailis

Khidmat: Service

khifa: Struggle

Khila: Robe of honor, distributed to emirs and ambassadors by medieval rulers as a mark of favor. On the shoulder they bore tiraz woven inscriptions in the ruler's name thus implying that the receiver was his servant.

Khilaaf: Controversy, dispute and discord.

Khilafah: Man's trusteeship and stewardship of Earth; Most basic theory of the Caliphate; Flora and fauna as sacred trust; Accountability to, God for harms to nature, failure to actively care and maintain. Three specific ways in which khalifa is manifested in Muslim practice are the creation of haram to protect water, hima to protect other species including those useful to man and by resisting infidel domination over Muslim lands in Jihad.

khimar: Another term used to describe the head covering worn by Muslim women

Khimar (pl. khumur): Islamic head covering (Q. 24:31).

Khirqa: Used cloth; (fig) cloak

Khitan: Male circumcision.

Khizr: The teacher of Moses in Quran 18:65-82, a saint who drank the water of life and lives among us, appearing occasionally as a spiritual guide

Khlafa or Rashidah: Rightly Guided Caliphs

Khojas: A division of the Ismailis

Khrijities (Khawarij): Those who refused recognition of the Shia'a and Sunni caliphs; they believed that the caliphate should be open to any Muslim of sound mind and body; "Those who withdrew"; one assassinated Ali, the 4th caliph, in Kufa, Iraq.

Khul: Divorce; instituted by a wife.

Khul: Renunciation or divorce initiated by the wife, according to the Shari'a. Signifies a woman's securing the annulment of her marriage through the payment of some compensation to her husband. A wife-initiated divorce.

Khulafa: Rashida

Khuluq: Ethics

Khums (Arabic: one fifth): Religious tithe applicable to Shia Muslims. One of the several duties incumbent upon Shias, khums, amounting to one fifth of a believer's raiding profits, should be used for charitable purposes. Fifth a tax of one fifth of all trading profits, payable to mujtahids in Shi'ite areas. literally one-fifth. One-fifth of the spoils of war is earmarked for the struggle to exalt the Word of God and to help the orphans, the needy, the wayfarer and the Prophet's kinsmen. Since the Prophet (peace be on him) devoted all his time to the cause of Islam, he was not in a position to earn his own living. Hence a part of **khums** was allocated for the maintenance of the Prophet (peace be on him) as well as for his family and the relatives dependent upon him for financial support. fifth

Khushu: Humility, devotion, concentration especially in prayer.

Khutba: A sermon delivered by an imam in the mosque, normally on Friday afternoon. The Friday sermon delivered in the great mosque of a town by the ruler or his legal representative which it was the duty of all adult Muslims to attend. Now essentially a moral discourse under the Umayyads and the early Abbasids its content was primarily political and the ceremonial which accompanied it was designed to show the prestige of the sovereign in state. The

134

sermon preached in the Mosque during the public communal prayer on Fridays. In early times, this was often a political statement made by or on behalf of the sovereign or administrative head of the area. Later, it became a predominately religious ceremony and was delivered by a preacher known as the Khatib.

Kibar: Old age

Kibr: Pride , arrogance

Kiraman Katibeen: The two angels assigned to each person that record good and bad deeds in our book of records.

Kirpau: Is a special kind of large dagger which is kept by the Sikhs for religious reasons

Kiswa: A black embroidered cloth which is draped over the Ka'aba, bearing Qur'anic verses.

Kiswa: A black silk curtain covering the Ka'aba.

Kiswa: Black clothing or covering of the Ka'ba renewed annually; the embroidered black cloth that covers the Ka'bah in Mecca.

Kiswah: Cover placed over the ka'abah

Kitab: The Book; the Meta-Book of all Divine Revelation, but also the Quran as the final form of that Book and therefore the most authoritative. Book, The Quran is often referred to as Al Kitab (the book). The book or religious scriptures, Umm al Kitab Mother of Scripture, divine text of which the Quran is part.

Kitabullah: "Book of God." One of the titles of the Qur'an.

Koran: (or Qur'an) The Holy Scripture of Islam. Muslim believe the Koran to be the word and will of God, as revealed to his messenger Muhammad (570-632) through the angel Jibril or Gabriel over the period 610-32. written in classical Arabic, it consists of 122 *suras* (chapters) of varying length, each *sura* being composed of a number of *ayas* (normally translated as verses because assonance is involved, although the Koran is a prose work). The first revelation on *Lailat al-Qadr,* the Night of Power, is commemorated during Ramadan (the ninth month of the Islamic calendar, devoted to fasting, almsgiving, and prayer). Since the Koran is regarded by Muslims as a literal transcription of God's revelations, for many years translations of the text were not permitted, and although today translations do exist, Muslims are taught to memorize and chant the original Arabic text. Calligraphic renditions of the text are a distinctive aid to worship in Islam. recitation or discourse; the Islamic holy book. (The Arabic spelling would be Qur'an' but it is spelled Koran in this book. The Westernized spelling makes it easier to read for English speakers.) literally, "the recitation"; the text of Muhammad's revelations and prophecies; the holy book of the Islamic faith.

Kufar: Plural version of *kafir*

Kufi: Islamic script; calligraphy. Islamic skullcap

Kufic: A square highly decorated Arabic scripts the origin of which is groundlessly attributed to Kufa in Iraq. It was much used for early Korans and for architectural inscriptions up to the early 13th century but it coexisted with rounded scripts even in the Umayyad period and survived the general adopting of thuluth or maskhi for the coinage, chancery documents and Korans. a type of Arabic script evolved in al-Kufa, Iraq, and still used for calligraphic ornamentation.

Kufic: Islamic script developed in Kufa, Iraq; used for earlier copies of the Qur'an.

Kufr: The rejection of faith in Allah after understanding the truth. Disbelieving in Allah, the *Rasul*, and the Qur'an; infidelity. Lit.: that which covers the truth. Also means ingratitude. Its original meaning is to conceal. This word has been variously used in the Quran to denote: 1) state of absolute lack of faith..2) rejection or denial of any of the essentials of Islam; 3) attitude of ingratitude and thanklessness to God; and 4) non fulfillment of certain basic requirements of faith. In the accepted technical sense, kufr consists of rejection of the Divine Guidance communicated through the Prophets of faith. In the accepted technical sense, kufr consists of rejection of the Divine Guidance communicated through the Prophets and Messengers of God. More specifically, ever since the advent of the last of the Prophets and Messengers. Muhammad rejection of his teaching constitutes Kufr

Kufrul-hukmi: Disbelief from judgment.

Kufrul-'Inaad: Disbelief out of stubbornness.

Kufrul-Inkaar: Disbelief out of arrogance and pride.

Kufrul I'raadh: Disbelief due to avoidance

Kufrul Istibdaal: Disbelief because of trying to substitute Allah's laws.

Kufrul Istihaal: Disbelief out of trying to make HARAM into HALAL.

Kufrul Jahli: Disbelief from not being aware of or not understanding.

Kufrul Juhudi: Disbelief from obstinacy after being presented with truth.

Kufrul Nifaaq: Disbelief from obstinacy after being presented with truth.

Kufrul-hukmi: Disbelief from judgment

Kufrus Istihzaha: Disbelief due to mockery and derision

Kumarbi: Chief god of the Hurrians, subject of the most important Hittite epic.

Kun: God's command to the universe "Be!" is sufficient to create it.

Kunya: Honorable nickname given to parents based on the name of their firstborn child.

Kurds: Kurds are members of an ethnic group that inhabit the Zagros and Taurus Mountains of southeastern Turkey, north western Iran, northern Iraq, and the adjacent areas in Syria and Nakhichevan. It was not until the seventh century AD that they embraced Islam. Like Persians, who also embraced Islam, they retained their languages, but unlike them, they remained predominantly Sunni. The

Kurdish general, Salal al Din (Saladin) Ayubi, overpowered the Shi Fatimud dynasty in Egypt and established the Ayubid dynasty (1169-1250). Since the Treaty of Sevres (1920) which specified an autonomous Kurdistan, was not ratified, and since the subsequent Treaty of Lausanne (1923) made no mention of it, the aspirations of Kurdish nationalists remained unfulfilled. See also Kurds in Iran, Kurds in Iraq, and Kurds in Syria.

Kursi: The Gnostic eye; the eye of light; the center of the forehead where the light of Allah's *Nur*, His resplendence, was impressed on Adam's forehead. Lit.: The seat of the resplendence of Allah; the Footstool of God, mentioned in the Quran as embracing the heavens and the earth, located cosmologically right below the arsh, the Throne of the Merciful

Kursl: Has been variously interpreted by Muslim scholars. In the opinion of the author, it signifies sovereignty, dominion and authority. As for other Muslim scholars some have considered it to signify God's knowledge. A number of scholars however consider the Kursi a reality rather than a mere figurative expression. These scholars emphasize however that both the nature and modality of God's Kursi are not known to man

Kuttab al-Wahy: The Prophet's secretary

Kuttab: Koranic school usually attended prior to the start of regular schooling.

La ilah illa Allah: There is nothing other than You, O God. Only You are Allah. There is only one Lord, one deity, one God. To accept this with certitude, to strengthen one's *iman*, or absolute faith, and to affirm this *kalimah* is the state of Islam. There are two aspects. *La ilah* is the manifestations of creation, or *sifat*. *Illa Allah* is the essence, or *dhat*. All that has appeared, all creation, belongs to *la ilah*. The One who created all that, His name is Allah. See also: *kalimah, dhikr*. There is no God but Allah. The most important expression in Islam. It is part of the first pillar of Islam. Also is the message of all the Prophets, such as Abraham, Moses, Jesus and Muhammad.

Labbayk Allahuma: God, I obey you (said during hajj)

Laghw: Dirty, false, evil vain talk

La'nah: Imploration for withdrawal of God's mercy

La'nat al-jahannam: The curse of hell

Labbayk Allahuma: Allah Here I am! Said during Hajj

Labid ibn Rabi: Greatest Arab poet of the day.

Laghw: Dirty, false, evil vain talk

Lam: The Arabic letter (), which correlates to the English consonant 'I'. In the transformed man of wisdom, *lam* represents the *Nur*, the resplendence of Allah. See also: *alif, mim*. (A) the Arabic letter (ل) which correlates to the English consonant 'I." In the transformed man of wisdom, **lam** represents the **Nur**, the resplendence of Allah. See also: **alif, mim.**

Laqab, The: An honorific or descriptive epithet, sometimes a nickname, often a title. In its original and simplest form, it is a nickname usually referring to a physical quality; e.g. at

Tawil, the tall; al A'war the one eyed; al Atrash the deaf. At a later date, Persian and Turkish laqabs are encountered, as well as Arabic; e.g. Jehangir, world seizer; Yildrim thunderbolt. Laqabs of a different character were adopted as throne names by reigning caliphs and sultans. Laqabs of honor were also given as titles to princes, statesmen, generals and high officers of state. These are usually compounds with din. ("faith). Or Dawla "state. E.g. Badr ad din "full moon of the faith, Jalal ad din Majesty of the faith, Siraj ad Dawla "lamp of the state.

Laylat al Qadr: The Night of Power, towards the end of Ramadan, when Muhammad received the first revelation of the Quran. "The Night of Measurement or Power." The exact date on which Muhammad started receiving the Qur'an. It falls in 1 of the last 10 days or Ramadan.

Lhilafa: Trusteeship.

Liwa: Means banner, flag, standard. In pre Islamic Makka, it was an honored function assigned to one of the clans of Quraysh to carry it which indicated its position of leadership in the battle.

Loya: National

Luqman: A prophet

Ma malakat aymanukum: One's rightful spouse (literally: what your right hand possess)

Ma na: Meaning the spiritual, intelligible, invisible dimension of a thing, contrasted with surat

Ma sha'a Allah: Whatever God has willed

Ma'araka: Battle

Ma'arri: Islam's most brilliant poet in medieval times.

Ma'rifa: Momentary experience of the Divine. Recognition, knowledge, gnosis, direct, spiritual perception as opposed to indirect knowledge or book learning; knowledge in general, especially in modern Arabic usage. In religious literature it means esoteric or mystical knowledge of God, gnosis.

Ma'rifah: "The eye of the heart" (Sufism)

Ma'ruf: Refers to the conduct which is accepted as good and fair by human beings in general. Consensus of the community. Known term used in the Quran for familiar and approved custom, hence generally the good.

Ma'shallah: "Whatever is the will of Allah."

Mabahidth/mubahas: Investigation

Madda: Matter

Madh'hab: School of law.

Madh'hab: School of religious jurisprudence, school of thought; ("chosen way"): one of the four legitimate schools of Islamic jurisprudence; a legal rite of the Shari'a.

Madhahib (pl. Madhhab): Schools; four major Islamic schools, named after their founders: Malikiyya, Hanifiyya,

Shafi'iyya, Hanbaliyya.

Madhhabs: Schools of law, all accepting the preeminence of the Koran and Tradition but differing in the emphasis in individual cases put upon sound judgment, consensus or common opinion, analogy or deduction and equity as means of reaching a correct verdict. In Sunni Islam there are now four main schools: Shafi'i, Hanafi, Maliki and Hanbali. School of religious jurisprudence, school of thought; ("chosen way"): one of the four legitimate schools of Islamic jurisprudence; a legal rite of the Shari'a.

Madhhah: School of jurisprudence, founded by Abu Hanifa.

Madinat al-Nabi: The City of the Prophet

Madinat Al-Salam: City of Peace; capital of Iraq.

Madmun: Convert to Islam

Madrasa: College for the teaching of theology and canon law. Early madrasas recorded in 10th century Khurasan were smaller normally grouped around a single teacher and were little different from teaching zawiyas in mosques. Under the Seljuks in Iraq and the Zengids in Syria madrasas became state institutions with salaried staff and students endowed upon the foundation but the primacy of Mosques as educational institutions was never lost; religious or theological school – traditionally the site in which the **ulama** was trained in Islamic law and doctrine; school, college, and esp. one of the Islamic learning. An Islamic school in which study centers on developing a profound knowledge of the Holy Qur'an, with students – *talib* in Arabic – often learning the text by heart.

Madrasah: Islamic school

Maghazi: Prophetic military campaigns

Maghreb: An Arabic term literally meaning "the place or time of sunset". It is used to denote the sunset prayer, and sometimes in the general sense of west or occident. Its most common use in Arabic is to denote the region of Muslim northwest Africa, including Morocco, Algeria, Tunisia and sometimes though not usually Libya.

Maghrib: The fourth *waqt* of the five-times prayer in Islam. Lit.: The time of sunset; also means the west. Literally the West. The lands of Islam, including Tunisia, Morocco, Algeria and Spain, regarded by the classical authors as peripheral to the course of Islamic history despite their considerable cultural contribution. One of the five prayers. The time for its performance begins with sunset and ends with the red glow of the sunset disappears. Sunset hence the prayer or salat at sunset, also Muslim occident, i.e., NW Africa, Morocco, for which the French translation Maghreb is commonly used. The fourth daily salat prayer

Magi: A priest; Zoroastrian. From Persian, pl, **magush,** a Zoroastrian priest; those who came to adore the infant Christ.

Mahabba: Love, the sole divine attribute that the Quran ascribes equally to man and God, He loves them and they love him. Mystical love (Sufism).

Mahabbat-E Kull: Universal love, Sufi

Mahdi (Arabic: The guided one, leader): The concept of mahdi, the Rightly Guided one, who will end injustice and restore faith while claiming divine sanction, is well defined in Judaism, Christianity and Twelver Shiism. Twelver Shias believe that the twelfth Imam Muhammad al Qasim, the infant son of the eleventh Imam Hassan al Askari, is their mahdi, who had been in spiritual occultation since AD 874 but will reappear to institute the rule of justice on earth before the Day of Judgment. The Islamic spiritual and temporal savior. According to Islamic teaching he will be sent by divine command to prepare human society for the end of earthly time by means of perfect and just government (Millenarianism). Many have claimed to be the Mahdi at different times, Best know was Muhammad Ahmad bin Abdallah (1843-85). Of Nubian origin, he claimed descent from Muhammad. Feeling called to purify the world from wantonness and corruption, he gathered many followers and proclaimed himself Mahdi in 1881. In 1882 he Egyptian government sent expeditions against him, but by 1884, with the capture of Khartoum, he made himself master of Sudan. General Gordon was killed in Khartoum on 30 January 1885; the Mahdi himself died, probably of typhus, five months later. Politically his struggle was carried on by the Khalifa Abdallah until Kitchener defeated him at Omdurman in 1898. "a guide". More specifically al Mahdi (the guide) is a figure who will appear with Prophet Jesus before the end of time, when God allows it, to bring world peace, order and justice, after it has been overcome with injustice and aggression. The Sunnis regard someone else as the Mahdi. According to Shiite belief, the 12th and last Imam, who has been hidden from humanity's view for centuries but will reappear to usher in a period of justice before Judgment Day. An Arabic term literally meaning "the rightly guided one," that is to say, "guided by God." According to a Muslim belief that is widely held though not grounded in the Koran, the Mahdi is a Messianic figure who will come at the end of time to establish justice and restore the faith. There have been many claimants to this title and office in the course of Muslim history. Awaited one, a Messiah and reformist leader who aims to restore the original purity of the Islamic faith and polity. In Shi'ite tradition the Twelfth Imam. Messiah who will come to restore religion and justice: twelfth imam expected by the Shiites

Mahdur ad Damm: He whose blood must be wasted

Mahl: Dowry, given to the bride.

Mahr: (bridal due) Signifies the amount of payment that is settled between the spouses at the time of marriage and which the husband is required to make to his bride. Mahr symbolized the financial responsibility that a husband undertakes towards his wife by virtue of entering into the contract of marriage. A gift a groom offers a bride. Dowry given to a woman on marriage and retained by her if she is divorced by her Husband. Sometimes loosely translated dowry. In Islamic law, the mahr is a kind of bridal gift given by the bridegroom to his bride, whose property it becomes. A mandatory gift given by a husband to his wife on their wedding day.

Mahram: A relative of the opposite gender usually described as being "within the forbidden limits"; a better description is "within the protected limits" means relatives who one can appear before without observing hijab and who one cannot marry.

Mahrim: A man barred from marrying a particular woman; (fig) male escort

Majaj: Magog (Bible)

Majalis: Assembly

Majallat: Review

Majlis I shura: Consultative council, parliament

Majlis: Assembly

Majnun: Crazy

Makhafa: Fear specifically for God

Makhpela: Cave; burial of Abraham and Sarah.

Makluq: Creator

Makr: Signifies a secret strategy of which the victim has no inkling until the decisive blow is struck. Until then, the victim is under the illusion that everything is in good order.

Makrooh (Makruh): Undesirable act or behavior; undesirable or doubtful things that are best to avoid. Means "detested", though not haraam (forbidden); something that is disliked or offensive. If a person commits the Makruh, he does not accumulate ithim but avoiding the Makhruh is rewarded with thawab. Acts of designated as distasteful or undesirable under Islamic law, there is merit in abstaining from them but no sin in committing them.

Maks: A tax not allowed by the Shari'a.

Maktab: School for the teaching of the Koran. Primary education in Islam was left to parents so that maktabs were often orphans. Even imperial maktabs like those founded by Ottoman sultans in the late 15th century were private, in the important sense that there was no control over teaching and the curriculum. Religious school.

Mala'ika: Angels

Mala'ikah (Mala eeka): Angels, beings with power, message-bearers. It was one of these mala'ika, Jibril who delivered Allah's revelation to Muhammad.

Malak: Means message bearer and is used in the Islamic texts for angels

Malakut: The spiritual realm, the imaginable realm

Malekite: One of the four juridical schools of Sunni Islam, prominent in North and West Africa

Malik Al Mulook: King of Kings

Malik El-Mawt: Angel of Death

Maliki code: Sunni Islamic school, the Maliki Code is the canonical school of Sunni Islam founded by Malik ibn Anas Ad 714-96, a jurist resident in Medina. Like other schools it is based on the Quran the sunna and ijma. The Maliki code's initial dominance of the Arab heartland of Islam gave way to the Shafii Code. The school of law founded by Malik b. Anas in which the principle of compromise was initially extremely important. It was chiefly established in the Maghrib and virtually all Islamic Africa including much of Upper Egypt. Referring to the Sunni Legal madhhab ascribed to Malik ibn Anasa; school of law founded by Malik ibn Anas (d.795). This school predominates in the Arab West and West Africa.

Malikul Mawt: The angel of death.

Ma malakat aymanukum: one's rightful spouse (literally: what your right hands possess)

Mamluk: Member of a military elite, originally a slave.

Manar: Tower

Manara: "A Place of Flames"; a tower from which Muslims are called to prayer (adjacent to a mosque).

Manasik: the rules specifying the requirements of a legally valid hajj.

Manat: Arabian god, deity. One of the goddesses worshipped by the pagan Quraysh

Mandub: Commendable or recommended. Failure to do it would not be a sin. (see halal mustahabb)

Manhaj: the methodology by which truth is reached

Manjum: Possessed by a jinn; crazy

Mansukh: That which is abrogated. The doctrine of al Nasikh wal Mansukh (abrogation) of certain parts of the Qur'anic revelation by others. The principle is mentioned in the Qur'an see maskh.

149

Mantiq: Logic

Manzil: One of seven equal parts of the Qur'an

Maqamat: Arabic literature. Stages of mystical experience (Sufi).

Maqasid: Goals or purposes; such as the purposes of Islamic law. Masaleh: public interests.

marakaz: Center

Maratib: Degrees, levels, of spirit or being

Mariyah or Marya or Meriem: Coptic concubine sent to Medina as a gift to the Prophet from Muqaqis, a ruler of Egypt. She was given her freedom after she gave birth to Muhammad's son Ibrahim, though she was never given the honor of being addressed like the Prophet's other wives as a Mother of the Faithful.

Marja e Taqlid (Persian: Source of Emulation): In Twelver Shiism the idea of a living mujtahid interpreting the Sharia took hold in the late eighteenth century. Muhammad Baqir Behbehani, a mujtahid based in Karbala ruled that every believer must choose a mujtahid to emulate who was given the honorific of marja-e taqlid. They carried the title of Grand Ayatollah. See also mujtahid and Titles, Religious (Shia Islam).

Marja: Source

Marja-I Taqlid (plural: **maraji-i taqlid**): 'source of imitation'. Title given to the most learned Shi'ite **mujtahids.**

Marja-Yi Mutlaq: The senior living **marja-I taqlid**, whose

Saul Silas Fathi

authority – if they agree who he is – is recognized by all Shi'ite **mujtahids.**

Markaz al-Islami: Islamic center

Markaz: Center

Martyr: Someone who dies for his or her religious, political, or moral beliefs. Originally meaning a legal 'witness', the term came to denote anyone who died for professing the Christian faith after St. Stephen, the first Christian martyr, was stoned to death in Jerusalem (c. 35). Martyrs ranked before all other saints, were venerated for their courage and faith, and were considered powerful intercessors between man and God. In Islam, the *shahid* ('witness') is a similar concept: those who die in a *jihad* or holy war are considered martyrs, and are guaranteed a place in heaven. Shiite Muslim regard the martyrdom of Husain (in 680 AD), commemorated on the holy day of *ashura*, as the turning-point in their history. Sikhs commemorate the martyrdoms of two of their Gurus, Arjan and Tegh Bahadur. In Judaism, the six million Jews murdered during World War II are remembered as Martyrs.

Ma'ruf: consensus of the community

Maruf: virtue

Mary the Copt: Muhammad's concubine and mother of his son Ibrahim, who died in infancy. **Maryam:** An Egyptian Coptic Christian, Muhammad's concubine.

Masha Allah: Allah has willed it.

151

Mashhad: "a place of witness" the equivalent of the Greek martyrdom applied to Shia shrines in particular whether or not their occupant is believed to have died a martyr.

Mashriq: Literally the East. The lands of the Eastern Caliphate in which Egypt and Syria were generally included as clients and protectors of the Abbasid caliphate. The Eastern frontier was conventionally accepted as Transoxania despite the presence of substantial Muslims communities in Turkistan and China. Sunrise: Levant.

Masih (Masceh): The Messiah. A term attributed to Jesus in the Qur'an. He was meant to be the Messiah for the Jewish people.

Masjid (plural: **masajid**): Place of prayer, mosque. "Place of prostration." The proper name for a Muslim house of worship. Place of prayer, prostration, hence Mosque. In early Islam there was no special term for Friday mosques. However later masjid was restricted to smaller oratories where the Friday prayer might not be said. In modern terminology masjid and musalla are virtually synonymous. *Mosque* is a word of French origin.

Masjid al Haram: "The Restricted Mosque." Another name for the Ka'bah and the mosque that surrounds it. Many restrictions apply upon a person who enters this mosque, such as the person must not kill any living thing, even a bug; and the person must be in a purified state; the area around the Kaaba

Masjid al-Aqsa: The Farthest Mosque, in Jerusalem

Masjid al-Nabawi: Mosque of the Prophet

Maslahah (Maslah): Beneficial. That which is beneficial, term used for the principle of public interest in the Maliki ,madhhab, adopted by modern legal reformers. The public welfare; the common good.

Math'hab: (pl. Madhahib) school of religious jurisprudence, school of thought; Mawali or mawala: Non-Arab Muslims

Mathnawi, The: The name of the collected poems of Jalaluddin Rumi. The greatest classic of the Sufi tradition

Matn: Text

Muadu: Fabricated

Maulana: Cleric or preacher

maulavi: Cleric or preacher

Maulid un Nabi: The birthday of the Prophet Muhammad. This widely celebrated holiday is controversial in Islam because it has no sanction from the main Islamic sources.

Maulid: Birthday, festival celebrating the anniversary of a religious figure.

Maulvi (maulana): A mullah

Maulvi: An honorific Islamic religious title often but not exclusively, given to Muslim religious scholars or Ulema preceding their names. Maulvi generally means any religious cleric or teacher.

Mawali (clients): Convert. The name given to the early non-Arab converts to Islam, who had to become nominal clients of one of the tribes when they became Muslims. Clients or associates. Non Arab Muslims. Associates, or clients, status at first given to non Arab converts in Islam. sing. Mawla: clients or associates. New-comers to Islam, converts, "clients", to distinguish them from the ruling Arab class.

Mawl'a al-Islam (A): Friends of Islam; master (lord) of Islam

Mawla: Pl. mawli, protector or supporter.

Mawlana: An Arabic word literally meaning "our lord or our master." It is used mostly as a title preceding the name of a respected religious leader, in particular graduates of religious institutions. The term is sometimes used to refer to Rumi.

Mawlanah: Our God

Mawlawi : A sheikh; a teacher; master; (A) a sheikh; a teacher; master.

Mawlid: The festival commemorating the birthday of a religious figure, usually a "saint." Another term used is **musim**

Mawlid an-Nabi: The Prophet's birthday

Maya: Illusion; the unreality of the visible world; the glitters seen in the darkness of illusion; the 105 million glitters seen in the darkness of the mind which result in 105 million rebirths. Maya is an energy, or **sakti**, which takes on various shapes, causes man to forfeit his wisdom, and confuses and hypnotizes him into a state of torpor. Maya can take many, many millions of hypnotic forms. If man tries to grasp one of these forms with his intellect, though he sees the form he will never catch it, for it will take on yet another form.

Maydan: An open space in a town, hence now a square. Few medieval Islamic towns had more than slight widening at crossroads where markets sometimes grew up. But the rulers palaces were often approached by a broad esplanade for example the 9th century Qaramaydan before Ibn Tulun's palace in Cairo.

Mazar-I-Sharif: The noble tomb, derived its name from the belief that the 4th of the rightly guided caliph, Ali, was buried there.

Mecca (*Makkah*): the holiest city in Islam

Medina (*Madīnah*): "city"; Medinat-un-Nabi means "the City of the Prophet." See Hijra
(Islam).

Me'raj: Muhammad's ascending to Heaven. The Night Journey.

Mevlud: Birthday, celebration of the birth of a saint

Mi raj ar ruhani: The spiritual ascent to God available to the Prophet's followers

Mi raj: Ascent, ladder, Muhammad's ascent through the seven spheres into the divine presence

Mi'ad: The resurrection, God will resurrect all of humankind to be judged. Shi'as regard this as the fifth Pillar of Islam.

Mi'raj (A): The night journey of the Prophet Muhammad through the heavens said to have taken place in the twelfth year of the Prophet's mission, on the 27th of the month of *Rajab*. During this event the divine order for five-times prayer was given. Lit.: an ascent. The ascent of the Prophet Muhammad to heaven and to the Lote Tree of the Limit in 619 CE, after his Night Journey from Mecca to Jerusalem (the isra). Ascent; Prophet Muhammad's journey to the Seven Heavens.

Mihna: Inquisition

Mihrab: A large decoration set in the wall of a mosque indicating the direction of the Ka'aba in Mecca.

Mihrab: An empty niche in the mosque, indicating the qibla, the direction of prayer. Niche or slab in place of prayer indicating the qibla or direction of Mecca. Its origins are disputed but by the reign of Abd al Malik a mihrab was installed underneath the Dome of the Rock and because standard features on Mosques, Masjids and madrasas.

Mika'il: The angel who can alter the weather by God's command.

Mikah: Marriage

Millah: In Arabic, millah means "religion," but it has only been used to refer to religions other than Islam, which is din.

Millat: Nation

Millet: In an Islamic state, "Ahl al Kitab" may continue to practice their former religion in a semi-autonomous community termed the millet.

Mim: The Arabic letter () which correlates to the English consonant 'm'. In the transformed man of wisdom, *mim* represents Muhammad. The shape of *mim* is like a sperm and from this comes the *nuqtah*, or dot, which is the form of the world. See also: *alif, lam*

Mina: A village near Mecca, part of the pilgrimage.

Minaret: In theory the tower from which the call to prayer was given five times a day. Hence an essential element of mosque architecture. Later though never solitary they were added to many private foundations-madrasas, khanqahs or mausolea. Their origins in Syria were probably square Roman watch towers. Tower from which the muezzin performs the call to prayer.

Minbar: A pulpit, in the form of a movable staircase, from which the **imam** preaches the Friday sermon, **khutbah;** a raised pulpit in the mosque where the Imam stands to deliver sermons. Pulpit from which the Friday prayer in a mosque is given. It owes its developments to Umayyad and early Abbasid ceremonial, but it may have been derived from bishops thrones like that of monastery of St Jeremiah at Saqqara. The earliest extant minbars are hollow paneled wood constructions. In Mamluk Cairo and Ottoman Turkey stone or marble was also used and there is a ceramic mosaic minbar at Kashan.

Minhaj: Methodology, e.g. methods, rules, system, procedures.

Miqat: Denotes the points which an outsider intending to perform Pilgrimage may cross only in the state of consecration. These points were fixed according to directions from God; intended place

Miraj: The night journey of the Prophet Muhammad through the heavens said to have taken place in the twelfth year of the Prophet's mission, on the 27th of the month of **Rajab.** During this event the divine order for five-times prayer was given. Lit.: an ascent. Literally meaning ladder refers to the miraculous nocturnal journey of the prophet from Jerusalem where he was taken during the night by God to the heavens. The ascension to Heaven that Muhammad made during his night journey to Jerusalem. The ascent of the Prophet Muhammad to heaven and to the Lote Tree of the Limit in 619 CE, after his Night Journey from Mecca to Jerusalem.

Miskin: Poor person; one who possesses no property at all. (pl. **masakin**) denotes helplessness, destitution. Thus **masakin** are those who are in greater distress than the ordinary poor people. Explaining this word the Prophet (peace be on him) declared that **masakin** are those who cannot make both ends meet, who face acute hardship and yet whose sense of self-respect prevents them from asking for aid from others and whose outward demeanor fails to create the impression that they are deserving of help.

Mithaq: Covenant

Mnuafiq: A hypocrite.

Mohammadanism: The name Europeans gave to the religion of Islam in the seventeenth century, thinking that Muslims worshipped Muhammad as god

Monsoon: A word borrowed from Arabic via India, where it was picked up and brought to Europe, first by the Portuguese and then by the Dutch, the French and other Western nations active in Asia in the 16th and 17th centuries. It comes from the Arabic word mawsim, which simply means season and was used to designate the periodic winds and heavy rainfall in the south Asian seas.

Mor: Ugaritic god of the rainless season and sterility, associated with the netherworld.

Moriscoes: Muslims who sailed with Columbus

Mosque: An Islamic place of public worship in Arabic, masjid (place of prostration). The first mosque built by the Prophet Muhammad (AD 570-632) at Quba near Medina was a simple courtyard. The head of a mosque is called imam and acts as the prayer leader. Sometimes he also acts as a religious instructor (maulawi). Muslims are required to pray collectively on Fridays, the Islamic holy day and the Friday prayer sermon is especially important. After the establishment of an Islamic republic in Iran, mosques were put to traditional use with neighborhood Revolutionary Komitehs basing themselves in mosques and conducting such state administration as issuing ration cards and recruiting volunteers to the Basij militia.

Mount Arafat: Pre-Islamic hajj 16 mi8les outside Mecca. The original covenant God made with Adam, the first prophet and the founder of the human race.

Mount Hira: (Cave). A mountain near Mecca where the cave "Hira" is situated.

Mu'adhdhin: Or muezzin. The individual who makes the call to prayer (see **adhan)** five times daily from the minaret of a mosque; the mosque leader who issues the call to prayer at various times each day.

Mu'ahadat: treaties

Mu'awwidhatayn: suras Al-Falaq and an-Nas, the "Surahs of refuge", should be said to relieve suffering (also protect from Black Magic)

Mu'min: A true believer; one of true *iman*, or absolute faith, certitude, and determination. The believer; one who professes belief in God, the Prophets and Judgment day; a member of the ahl al kitab. A Muslim who observes the commandments of the Quran

Mu'min: A believer

Mu'tawwif: Guide caring for pilgrims in Makka.

Mu'tazilis: (Mu'tazilites) Those who stand aloof, theologians belonging to the rationalist school which introduced speculative dogmatism into Islam. Islamic theological school; started about 2 decades before the coming of the Abbasids; eventually rejected. Moderate withdrawers

Muadhin: A caller to prayer, men only.

Mubaah: Permitted.

Mubah: Acts allowed under Islamic law, commission or omission of which are not sins.

Mubaligh: Person who recites the Quran

Muban: literally permissible; neither forbidden nor commended. Neutral. (See halal)

Mubarak: Blessed

Mubarakat: Blessings; the supreme, imperishable treasure of all three worlds (*al-awwal, dunya,* and *al-akhirah*)

Muezzin: Caller-to-prayer

Muezzin: The official on the staff of a pious foundation charged with giving the call to prayer five times a day. Most foundations had two but the mosque madrasa of Sultan Hasan in Cairo had a whole chorus of muezzins.

Mufa'khathat: placing between the thighs

Mufsidun: Evil doer a person who wages jihad not in accordance with the Qur'an. Plural mufsideen.

Mufti: A learned Islamic leader who gives or is qualified to give Islamic verdicts; **alim** appointed by the government to give official rulings on Islamic law. An Arabic word literally meaning " one who is competent to issue a fatwa." The mufti was originally a kind of freelance jurisconsult. In Ottoman times, it became the common practice to appoint a mufti to a city, district or province, as chief authority in the area in matters concerned with the holy law of Islam, the Shari'a. This practice was retained in the post Ottoman states of the Middle East.

Mughal: Rulers of India, descendants of Timur and Genghis Khan.

Mughals: Islamic dynasty in India. King Shah Jahan built the Taj Mahal at Agra (1630-1648) for his wife who died giving birth to their son,

Mumtaz Mahal.

Mughals: The word of "Mongols" in Persian; related to the Turks.

Muhaddithun: Scholars of hadith

Muhaiyaddeen or *Muhyiddin*: The pure resplendence called the *Qutb*. The one who manifests the wisdom which lies hidden and buried under illusion (maya). The one who gives life to that wisdom and shows it again as a resplendence. The one who revives the life of wisdom and gives it to someone else. *Muhaiyaddeen*: *Mu* is that which existed earlier; *hay* is life, *ya* is a title of greatness, a title of praise; and *din* means the light which is perfectly pure. *Din* is what existed in the beginning, the 'ancient thing' which was with God originally and is always with Him. To that purity God gave the name *Muhaiyaddeen*. *Muhaiyaddeen* is that beauty which manifested from Allah and to which Allah gave His *wilayat* [powers]. Lit.: the giver of life to the true belief

Muhajabah: Woman who wears hijab (polite form of hijabi).

Muhajirin: (Muhajirun) Those who emigrated from Makka to Medina with Muhammad. See also Hijra. Migrants, those who made the Hijra. The first Muslims that accompanied Muhammad when he traveled to Medina.

Muhakkamat: unequivocal verses of Qur'an. (See mutashebehat.)

Muham (T): Face or countenance. Muhammad can be defined as the beauty of the heart [*aham*] reflected in the face

Muhammad al-Ummi: The unlettered Muhammad

Muhammad ibn Abdallah: The prophet of Islam, Muhammad.

Saul Silas Fathi

Muhammad Mustafa al-Rasul : *Mustafa* – the chosen one; *al-Rasul* – the Messenger. A name used for Prophet Muhammad

Muhammad: According to Islam, The Last Prophet of God, directed to deliver the Final Book (itself a portion of the Meta Book or umm al Kitab in Arabic to Arabs but with a message encompassing all humankind and all areas of history. (c. 570-632) the Prophet of Islam. He was born in Mecca of the Hashemite clan of the tribe of Quarish and orphaned in infancy. He won the name 'al-Amin', 'the trustworthy', and married his employer a wealthy widow, Khadija. Religious contemplation led him to a vision on the 'Night of Power' in 610 and to the revelations that were subsequently compiled as the Koran. From 613 he preached openly against idolatry and the social evils of his day, proclaiming the oneness of Allah, 'the God', and the inevitability of judgment. The death of Khadija and of his protective uncle Au Talib in 619 exposed the Prophet and his followers to the hostility of the Meccans and led ultimately to his departure from Mecca (the Hegira) of 622 and the establishment of the first community of Muslim at Medina. A lengthy period of sometimes violent struggle followed, ending in the capitulation of Mecca to Muhammad and his followers, the purgation of the Kaaba of idols, and the submission to Islam of most of the tribes of the Arabian peninsula. The Prophet's sudden death in 632 led to the establishment of the Caliphate and indirectly inaugurated the tide of Arab Conquests.

Muhammadan: A name often used incorrectly by non-Muslims in referring to followers of Islam (Muslims). The term is unacceptable to Muslims, for it implies that their worship and religion revolve around the man Muhammad.

163

Muhammadun rasulullah: Muhammad is the messenger of God. This statement is the second part of the first pillar of Islam. This is the second most important statement in Islam.

Muharakat: Blessings; the supreme, imperishable treasure of all three worlds (**al-awwal, dunya** and **al-akhirah**).

Muharebeh: a person who wages war against God

Muharram: First Islamic month in which Imam Hussain was martyred at Karbala. Islamic month.

Muhartiq: Heretic.

Muhsanat: Means protected women. It has been used in the Quran in two different meanings. First is has been used in the sense of married women that is, those who enjoy the protection of their husbands. Second, it has been used in the sense of those who enjoy the protection of families as opposed to slave girls.

Muhsin: A person who performs a good deed. Plural muhsineen. Opposite of Mufsidun.

Muhtasib: Enforcer of regulations in the market place; inspector. Legal official appointed to oversee the markets as inspector of weights and measures and controller of prices. He was also a censor of public morals and was empowers t demolish unsafe houses, repair or claim our foul water supplies and keep the streets of souqs clear.

Mujaddid: Renewer of the faith, said to come once in each century. Religious regenerator.

mujahdeen: Combatants in a jihad, name of various militant

Saul Silas Fathi

groups, especially in Iran and Afghanistan and of armed Islamic formations

Mujahedin (sing. Mujahid): Those who conduct jihad; Persons who wage jihad. May also be referred to as *jihadis.*

Mujahid: (pl. **mujahidin):** Soldier of God. Soldier fighting a holy war or jihad.

*Mujahideen***:** Arabic for "those who strive"; a term used to refer to holy warriors engaged in battles throughout the world to advance their vision of Islam

Mujtahid: (*Arabic: one who strives*) A mujtahid is one who practices Iijihad and the term applies to both Sunni and Shia clerics. In Twelver Shiism, the idea of a living mujahid interpreting the Sharia took hold in the late 18th century. In the Shia world the honorific "mujtahid" was replaced by "ayatollah" around the time of the 1907-11 Constitutional Revolution in Iran. In 2000 there were twenty-seven ayatollahs in that country. A jurist who has earned the right to exercise **ijtihad (q.v.),** usually in the Shii world. A person qualified to undertake **ijtihad.** A scholar who uses reason for the purpose of forming an opinion or making a ruling on a religious issue. Plural: Mujtahidun. A Shi'i cleric recognized as competent to deliver independent opinions on matters relating to the *Shari'a.* Muslim scholars qualified to use their knowledge of the Holy Qur'an as a source for legal decisions.

Mukhabarat: (*Arabic" lit., intelligence; fig., organization collection information*) Mukhabarat is the popular term used in Arab countries for the intelligence apparatus both at home and abroad. In addition, there is *Amn al Askariya*

(Arabic: Military Security). The generic term Mukhabarat covers up to five intelligence agencies.

Mukhtar: An Arabic word literally meaning "chosen." In the 19th century, the term was adopted in the Ottoman Empire to designate the headman of a village or of a city neighborhood. The mukhtar, who was almost invariably a local man, served in many ways as a link between the people and the central government. At some times and places the mukhtar was chosen locally, by some form of election, or, more precisely, consensus among the local leading families. At other times, more especially with the process of modernization, he was appointed from above, the system continued in many of the successor states after the breakup of the Ottoman empire.

Mulk: Dominion or existing Muslim state as distinct from the ideal Islamic state; kingdom, the universe, the corporeal world

Mullah or Mollah: A Persian word derived from the Arabic mawla which among many other meanings was used in the sense of the lord, master or patron. In this sense, it has been used politically such as in Morocco, where many of the sultans prefixed the word mawlay, "my master," to their names and religiously especially in Iran, for religious teachers and leaders. It is often used in Iran and in some other places to designate professional men of religion in general. (from **mawla** – 'lord'): a lesser member of the **ulama** (q.v.). Islamic clergy. Ideally they should have studied the Quran, Islamic traditions (hadith), and Islamic law (fiqh.)

Mumin: A true believer; one of true **iman,** or absolute faith, certitude, and determination. The believer; one who professes belief in God, the Prophets and Judgment Day; a member of the ahl al-kitab. **Muminin:** believers

Munafiq: Hypocrite; (fig) a deviant Muslim; Plural: Munafiqun

Munafiqin: Hypocrites

Munahhema: Comforter

munazamat: Organization minkar: vicegerent muqawama: resistance

Munkar: One of the two angels who interrogate a soul in the grave. (*See* also Nakir.) Unknown term used in Quran for wrongful action as distinct from ma ruf hence evil generally. Vice

Munsif: Subordinate judge

Muntaqabah: Pl. muntaqabat: woman who wears niqab.

Muqarnas: Honeycomb-like Islamic architecture.

Muqawama: Resistance

Muqri: Aspirant or follower of a Sufi master.

Murabaha: A type of sharia-compliant cortgage. (see Ijara)

Murjites: A school

Murjites: Religious school

Murshid: a Sufi teacher

Murtadd: Female apostate is Murtadah, apostate (see irtidad seee mahdur ad damm.)The technical Islamic term for an apostate, that is one who has renounced Islam. According to the holy law as traditionally understood, this is a capital offense and the offender must be put to death whatever the circumstances. Even if he later repents and reverses his apostasy he must still be executed. God may forgive him but no human authority is empowered to so. This penalty applies even in the case of a new convert to Islam, of however brief duration, who reverts to his previous faith. The death penalty normally included not only the convert but also anyone responsible for converting him. According to the proponents of taqiya the apostate may be forgiven if his apostasy is forced and false. In addition to a formal renunciation of the faith, some actions, such as certain forms of blasphemy are considered tantamount to apostasy ad incur the same penalties. Despite the impossibility of even attempting to convert Muslims, Christian missions of various churches were extremely active under some Muslim governments, notably under the Ottoman Empire. Their purpose was to convert Jews to Christianity and more especially to convert Christians from one church to another. During the long and bitter struggle between Protestants and Catholics in Europe both sides became aware that there was a large untapped reservoir of Christians in the Islamic lands, not committed to either of the contending Western churches. Most of the Middle Eastern Christians belonged to one or other of the Eastern churches-Orthodox, Armenian, Coptic, Syrian. For awhile Catholic missions achieved some success in supporting or creating Uniate churches, that is, autonomous churches with their own rules and rites but in communion with Rome. The best known of these is the Maronite church of Lebanon. The Protestant missions also succeeded in winning converts from among the Eastern churches. Under the rule of the Western Empires, the missionaries had free reign. Since the ending of Western imperial rule, their activities had been more circumscribed and in some countries in accordance with the old laws, totally forbidden. In general by conversion to Islam and migration the ancient Christian communities of the Middle Easy have been dwindling steadily.

Muruwah: Manliness

Muruwah: Muhammad's moral system

Muruwwa: Manly virtues

muruwwa: notion of manhood, code of honor, in Arab tradition

Musa: Moses

Musavat: Unity

Musbaha (Tasbeek): Muslim beads used in reciting words of remembrance (Catholic rosary beads); 99 beads, for 99 names of God, or 33 beads.

Mushaf: A copy, codex or redaction of the Quran. Original copy of the Qur'an.

Mushrik: A polytheist or disbeliever in the Oneness of Allah; person who does not believe there is only one God; An idolater. One who associates others in worship with God, a polytheist.

Mushrikoon: Idol worshippers, pagans.

mushrikoon: Pagan

Muslim Calendar: The: Muslims like Christians, created a new
calendar with a new era, beginning with the founder of
their faith. Unlike the Christians however they did not date
it from the birth of the Prophet Muhammad but from his
migration from Mecca to Yathrib, later known as Medina.
The Arabic name for the migration is Hijra, in English,
commonly misspelled Hegira. According to traditional
accounts, the Prophet left Medina on the date
corresponding to 16 July 622 and arrived in Medina on 22
September of the same year. The Muslim calendar, dating
from the beginning of the Arab year in which the Hijra took
place, was formally promulgated by the second caliph,
Umar, some 17 years later and has been universally used in
the Muslim world ever since. The Hijra is seen as an epoch-
making event and the dawn of a new era. Unlike Christians,
Muslims did not usually reckon backward as well as
forward from the beginnings of their era. There is no
accepted Muslim equivalent of the Western system of
dating known as BC= Before Christ, or more recently BCE
Before the Common Era. From early times, this calendar
posed some problems. The Muslim year is purely lunar,
consisting of 12 months, each containing 29 or 30 days.
The year is thus approximately 11 days shorter than the
solar year. Unlike the Jews and the Christians the Muslims
did not adopt the corrective of leap years, with the result
that in the course of a century, the individual months and
therefore al the feasts and fasts of the calendar, rotate
through all the solar seasons. Muslims, like others,
accepted the ancient divisions of the day into 24 hours. In
traditional Muslims usage, however, the day did not begin
at midnight, as in the Western world, but from sunset as in
the ancient and still current Jewish traditions. Muslims

have disagreed in the past as to whether the beginning and end of the day should be determined by calculation or by observation. The beginning of the 15th century of the Muslim era, that is the first day of the first month of the year 1400, corresponded to 21 November 1979. The year 1430 of the Hijra begins on 29 December 2008 CE. Since the Muslim lunar year does not correspond to the seasons, and since the government finances for so long depended on such seasonal matters as the harvest, it was found necessary from an early date to use other calendars for fiscal and more generally for bureaucratic purposes. Sometimes these were the pre existing solar calendars, Christian and other, in the countries that embraced Islam, sometimes they were solar adaptations of the Islamic calendar. The most important of these is the Iranian solar era, introduced in 1925. The numbering is based on the Hijra, but it is calculated in solar years, using an adaptation of the old pre Islamic Iranian month names. This era is now used in Iran for most purposes other than purely religious, for which the Hijra calendar is used and international for which the Common Era is used. The Iranian New Year, the first day of the first month of Farvardin, falls in the third week of March. To convert the Iranian solar year to the Common Era, add 622 to dates from 1 January to 21 March, and 621 to dates from 21 March to 31 December.

Muslim: The collector of an authoritative anthology of hadith reports. (Mus lim): " a person who is surrendering to God and finding peace." Any inherent to Islam. A follower of the religion of Islam. (noun): an adherent of Islam; (adj.): pertaining to Muslims. Member of the ummah, or worldwide community of Muslims.

Muslim: Imam, a Muslim scholar

Musta'liq: Arabic script which combined the Arabic Naskhi and the Persian Ta'liq into a beautiful light, legible script.

mustadafeen: The disinherited

Mustafa al-Rasul **(A):** The chosen Messenger

Mustahab: Desirable act or behavior.

Mustahabb: Commendable or recommended. (*see* halah, mandub)

Mustazafin: The wretched les miserable impoverished inhabitants of Iranian shanty towns.

Mut'ah: Literally joy; a type of temporary marriage practiced only by the Shi'ah, or a practice between Umrah and Hajj. Shi'ite legal institution of temporary marriage contract.

Mutashabehat: equivocal verses of Qur'an (See Muhakkamat.)

Muta'sibun: Fanatics

Mutawatir: "Agreed upon" used to describe hadith that were narrated by many witnesses through different narration chains leading back to Muhammad.

Mutaween, Singular. Mutawa: Religious police

Mutawiyin: Volunteers, enforcers of Wahhabism in Saudi Arabia

Mutayyabun: The scented ones

Mutazilab: (Arabic) the Muslim sect which attempted to explain the Koran in rational terms.

Mutazilis: Rationalists.

Mutazilite: An extreme conservative sect in early Islam.

Muttawin (sign. Muttawi): (lit) One who enforces compliance; (fig) religious policemuwahhidin (sing.) muwahhid): Unitarians

Muwahhid: Unitarian, one who believes in God's unity. Term used by Wahhabis and Druzes to describe their beliefs.

Muwahhidun: (Arabic: Unitarianism): See Wahhabism and Wahhabis.

Muwashshah: Arabic poetry

Muzdalif: The abode of the thunder god

Nabi: A prophet, one whose prophethood consists of receiving a direct message from God Almighty directed to the people with whom the prophet identifies, most often as a warner of impending calamities or a reminder of duties neglected; a prophet from God. Literally, prophet. In the Islamic context, a Nabi is a man sent by God to give guidance to man, but not given scripture. The Prophet Abraham was a nabi. This is in contrast to Rasul, or Messenger. Plural: Anbiya. See : Rasul. Prophet; a recipient of a communication from God intended for a specific community.

Nabidh: An Arabian wine; a mild fermented beverage made from raisins or dates mixed with water, later forbidden for Muslims.

Nadhir: The warner

Glossary of Arabic Terms

Nadir: A Jewish tribe of Medina; Muhammad besieged and exiled themselves Nakhla: An Arabian town where the Muslims carried out their first military raid against the Quraysh

Nafas ar Rahman: The Breath of the Merciful, the cosmos as the infinite words of God articulated within His own breath

Nafila: An optional, supererogatory practice of worship, in contrast to farida

Nafl: Prayer is a voluntary prayer an act of supererogatory devotion

Nafs **or** *nafs ammarah* **(A):** The seven kinds of base desires. That is, desires meant to satisfy one' own pleasure and comforts. All thoughts are contained within the *ammarah*. *Ammarah* is like the mother while the *nafs* are like the children. Lit.: person; spirit; inclination or desire which goads or incites toward evil. Breath, soul, conscience. Self, soul, used without qualification in Sufism, it means the ego, the negative tendencies that pull us away from God; typically understood as having several stages of growth leading to perfection; soul, one's self; Islamic term for the **id**, or self. The real you; your personality and character.

Nahjul Balagha: Path of eloquence

Najasah: Impurity

Najasat, Najis: An unclean thing

Naji: Impure

Nakir and Munkar: two malaikah who test the faith of the dead in their graves.

Naksat: Twelve animals representing months of the year.

Naqira: Speck on the back of a date stone.

Narghile: *See* Hookah

Nasab: Family, lineage, descent. Pedigree: among the father and a variable list of ancestors, each name being introduced by the word ibn, "son of." This is also written bin and ben and is often abbreviated to b. The feminine is bint. Writers may quote as many generations as they feel to be necessary, and in extreme cases, will go all the way back to Adam. The usual practice is to give one or two; e.g. Ali b. Muhammad b. Ahmed= Ali son of Muhammad, son of Ahmad. It is not uncommon for an ancestor in the list to be mentioned by a name other than his Ism; e.g. Ali b. Abi Talib= Ali the son of Abu Talib (the father of Talib). .

Nasara: The Islamic term for Christian. It comes from the name Nazareth. It is also related to the term for **helper**, which is how Jesus' disciples are viewed in the Qur'an .

Nasheed: Islamic songs relating to God's guidance.

Nasi: Was practiced in vogue among the pre Islamic Arabs: they altered the duration of the four sacred months. Whenever they wished to start fighting or to loot and plunder and they could not do so during the sacred months they carried out their expedition in one of the sacred months and then later on compensated for this violation by treating one of the non sacred months as a sacred month. It was practiced by the Arabs in two ways; (1) In order to shed blood or to plunder, or to satisfy a blood vendetta; here they declared a sacred month to be an ordinary one, and compensated for this violation later on by declaring one of the ordinary months to be sacred. (2) With a view to harmonizing the lunar calendar with the solar calendar the Arabs used to add a month to the lunar calendar. Their purpose in so doing was to ensure that the **Hajj** dates should consistently fall in the same season so that they were spared the hardship and inconvenience resulting from observation of the lunar calendar for the fixation of the **Hajj** dates.

Nasiha: Advice

Naskh: Islamic script used in writing the Qur'an. The doctrine of al Nasikh wal Mansukh (abrogation) of certain parts of the Qur'anic revelation by others. The principle is mentioned in the Qur'an (2:106) see mansukh. System of Qur'anic interpretation where new verses override previous verses

Naskhi: Islamic script developed by the famous scribe Ibn Al-Bawwab (rounded and cursive) used for letters and business documents.

Nasr: Help

Nass: A known, clear legal injunction. Designation of a successor, in particular a spiritual successor in the Shi'ite tradition.

Nifaq: Falsehood, dishonesty

Nifas: The bleeding after childbirth (see Haid)

Nifaz: Establishment

Night of Power (Laylat Al-Qadr): Free journey to God is established by two formative events: The "Night of Power" when God sent down the Qur'an to Muhammad, and the

176

"Night Journey" (Isra), also known as the "Ascent" (Mi'raj), when Muhammad rose up to his Lord.

Night of Power: One of the last ten nights of the month of Ramadan, in which the Koran descended onto the Preserved Tablet.

Nikah: The Islamic marriage ceremony.

Niqab: A kind of veil worn by Sunni Women influenced by the Muslim Brotherhood, the Salafiyya, and the Wahhabis. Only the eyes show, but there is a piece of material on top of the head so if the woman wishes to cover her eyes she can pull it down over them. Veil covering face; garment worn by Muslim women that include a face covering and gloves

Nisba, The: An adjective, usually derived from the place of birth, origin or residence, sometimes from the sect, tribe or family and occasionally from a trade or profession. A man may, thus have several nisbas, as al Qurashi al Hashimi al Baghdadi as Sayrafi "of the tribe of Quraish, of the house of Hashim, of the city of Baghdad, the money changer. In Arabic the Nisba is almost always preceded by the definite article and ends in i. Among the Turks the place Nisba with the ending li is normally placed at the beginning of a name; e.g. Ismirli Ali Riza, the Symrnoit Ali Riza. The nisba may be arbitrarily handed down from father to son, thought he original relevance is lost.

Niyazi Misri: Sufi Order

Niyya: Declaration of intention to carry out a religious responsibility, as in **salat**, or prayer, in the right spirit of mind and heart.

Niyyah: (Niyyat) "intention" necessary for the proper completion of a ritual, such as prayer

Nizari Islamis: A violent sect that plagued the Abbasid caliphs; an offshoot of the Shia, also known as "The Assassins".

Noble Qur'an: The name by which the Quran is best known reflecting both its message and source, since one of the Divine Names—as also one of the traits of the Prophet Muhammad—is noble.

Noble Sanctuary: Islamic site in Jerusalem. Built on Mount Moriah in the Old city of Jerusalem, the Noble Sanctuary, which houses the Dome of the Rock and al Aqsa Mosque (The distant Mosque) and measures 35 acres/0.14 sq km takes up about a third of the Muslim Quarter, which occupies nearly two fifths of the historic Old City. Al Aqsa Is a plainer, traditionally built mosque. It has prayer niches dedicated to Moses and Jesus. Following the annexation of East Jerusalem by Jordan, The Jordanian monarch acquired the custody of the Noble Sanctuary in 1950. When Israel occupied East Jerusalem in June 1976, it accepted the Jordanian custodianship. This was confirmed by the Jordanian Israeli Peace Treaty, which was signed in October 1994 and hotly disputed by the Palestine Liberation Organization.

Non-fundamentalist: In modern times, a traditionalist, a reformist, or a secularist.

Nubuwwa: Prophecy, a key principle of Islamic belief; prophet hood. Shi'as regard this as the third Pillar of Islam.

Nukra: A great munkar prohibited, evil, dreadful thing.

Nur **(A):** Light; resplendence of Allah; the plenitude of the light of Allah which has the brilliance of a hundred million suns; the completeness of Allah's qualities. When the plenitude of all these becomes one and resplends as one, that is the *Nur* – that is Allah's qualities and His beauty. It is the resplendent wisdom which is innate in man and can be awakened; light. Muslims believe angels were created from light and jinn from fire.

Nur: Light. Muslims believe angels were created from light and jinn from fire. Inner light (divine).

Nusairis: see Alawis.

Nusuk: Signify ritual sacrifice as well as other forms of devotion and worship.

Nut: The Egyptian sky goddess; wife and sister of Seb, and mother of Osiris and Isis. Member of the Great Ennead.

Nutfah: Mixed male and female sexual discharge; semen drops

Original Sin: Ghaflah

PLO: Palestinian Liberation Organization; founded in 1964 by Israel's enemy Arab States.

Paradise: From the Greek paradiesos, used by Xenophon to describe the parks and gardens of the kings of Persia, derived from the ancient Persian pairidaeza, an enclosed area. The term is applied in the Bible to the Garden of Eden, and more broadly to the abode of the blessed in heaven. The usual Arabic term is janna, literally garden.

The delights of paradise for males are describes in some detail in the Koran (52,55,56,76,ect.) and in still greater and more explicit detail in the early traditions and commentaries. The Koranic paradise has lush and bountiful gardens with rivers of wine and honey and milk, and water flowing constantly. Trees without thorns bear a multitude of flowers and fruits and their shade is long extended. The blessed will recline on thrones with green cushions, resting on beautiful carpets lined with rich brocade. They will wear garments of silk, have vessels of silver and crystal goblets and the cups will be full. Never will they suffer from indigestion or drunkenness. They will be attended by houris, chastes maidens who restrain their glances, and whom no man or genie has touched before them and also by youths "like hidden pearls."

parcham: Flag

Pardah: Veil; could be in the form of scarf or sheet in order to maintain modesty (also see **chador** and **hijab**)

Partisans of Ali: Shiah. Ali's supporters for his caliphate following Muhammad's death in 632 ACE (Muhammad's cousin and son-in-law).

Pasdaran: Guardians of the Islamic Revolution

Pashtun: Afghani tribe and language.

P.B.U.H.: an acronym that stands for "peace be unto him" a blessing which is affixed to Muhammad's name whenever it is written. In some circles and English writings, Sufis

180

regard PBUH to signify "Peace and Blessings Upon Him"
(the Rasul or Messenger of
Allah). These are the primary English explications of the
P.B.U.H. acronym. The
Arabic version is S.A.W.

Peshmerga: Literally, 'those who face death'; term referring to
Kurdish guerrilla forces.

Pilgrimage: A journey, usually lengthy, to visit a religious shrine
or site and undertaken as an act of religious devotion or
penance. Most religions have pilgrimage sites, such as
sacred rivers, shrines, or buildings, which have traditional
religious significance. Christian pilgrimage was initially
made to sites connected with the life of Jesus Christ in
Palestine (principally Jerusalem, also a sacred site for Jews
and Muslims), and Muslim obstruction of this custom
helped to provoke the Crusades. Pilgrimage to the Kaaba
at Mecca, well established in pagan Arabia, was
incorporated into Islam, the detailed rites being based on
Muhammad's own practice. Every Muslim tries to
undertake the pilgrimage (*hajj* in Arabic) to Mecca at least
once in a lifetime. The *hajj,* undertaken only in the twelfth
month of the Muslim calendar, became highly organized,
with special caravans and guides. The cities of Karbala and
Najaf in Iraq are sacred to Shiite Muslims.

Pir: (Arabic) The spiritual director of Muslim mystics. a Sufi
(q.v.) master, who can guide disciples along the mystical
path. Sufi master; the Persian word for shaikh

Poll tax: A*n across-the-board tax on every member of the group*
To keep the Arab conquerors separate from the conquered
people, the early caliphs of the Umayyad period (AD 661-

750) confined their soldiers to garrison towns.

Polygyny (Polygamy): The custom of having more than one wife at a time.

Polytheism: Belief in and worship of more than one god.

Prayer: There are three types of Islam: **duah, salat,** and **zikr.**

Prophet(s): There are two classes: **rasool** (messenger or envoy), who brings a new religion or major revelation, and **nabi** (prophet), whose mission lies within the framework of an existing religion. A messenger appointed by Allah to invite a community to believe in Him; one who speaks on God's behalf.

Purdah: Female seclusion a Persian word denoting the modest dress of women and the separation of women and men (mostly in India).

Pyramid: A monumental structure especially characteristic of ancient Egypt, often built as a royal tomb and usually made of stone, with a square base and sloping sides meeting centrally at an apex. At first the pharaohs were buried in underground chambers over which were built rectangular *mastabas*, stone structures housing the food and accoutrements the pharaoh would need in the afterlife. The first pyramid was that constructed for King Zoser at Saqqara by Imhotep in about 2700 BC the so-called Step Pyramid which has six enormous steps and is over 60 m (197 feet) high. A pyramid built at Meydum in about 2600 was originally of similar design, but the steps were later filled in with limestone to produce the classical pyramid shape. Most of the best known pyramids date from the Old

Saul Silas Fathi

Kingdom of the best known pyramids date from the Old Kingdom (c. 2700 – 2200 BC), though some were built during the 11th and 12th dynasties (c. 2050-1750 BC). The pyramids of Khufu, Khafre and Menkaure at Giza are a spectacular illustration of the skill of Egyptians architects and of the state's ability to organize a large workforce. The Great Pyramid of Giza, constructed of enormous stone blocks of up to 200 tons in weight, is estimated to have required a labor force equivalent to about 84,000 people employed for 80 days a year for 20 years.

Qa'a: Central reception hall with one, two or four iwans of Cairene palaces, the central space normally being covered. The Muslim topographers use qa'a in the sense of complete palace.

Qaabat al-Sakhra: Dome of the Rock

Qabd: see bast

Qada: "Determination." Often mistranslated as fatalism.

Qadar: Decrees

Qadar: Fate; predestination

Qadhf: False imputation of unchastely specifically punished by sharia

Qadi: Muslim judge mostly on points of religious law. It was customary for each madhhab to have its own qadi since a judge is bound to adhere to the decisions of his own school of law. Qadis although important urban notables rarely received large salaries but instead received most of their

183

income from administering trusts acting as executors and giving private legal opinions. Sometimes transcribed Kadi, a judge in a court of Islamic law. The judge in a Shar'i court. Male or female.

Qadi al-Qudat: Chief justice

Qadiri: A Sufi order

Qadiriyha: Scholarship

Qadiriyya: A group of Muslim scholars

Qadiriyyah: Sufi order (mysticism)

Qadr: "Measurement." Often mistranslated as destiny or fate. God's measurement of man.

Qaf: A mythic mountain, said to surround the world

Qaida: base

Qaimaqam: district governor; subordinate to governor of a province

Qalam: The pen with which God is said to have prerecorded the actions of men. The Prophet said the first thing which God created was the pen [*qalam*] and that it wrote down the quantity of every individual thing to be created, all that was and all that will be to all eternity. Lit.: a reed pen

Qalandariyya: Wandering dervishes without fixed abode strangely shaven and beringed whose coarse garments and unconventional behavior provoked astonishment in Damascus in 1213 and subsequently much disapproval.

They practiced physical mortification but were slack in their observances and were held to be immoral both by the orthodox ulama and by other orders of Sufis.

Qalb : The heart within the heart of man; the innermost heart. There are two states for the *qalb*. One state is made up of four chambers which are earth, fire, air, and water, representing Hinduism, Fire Worship, Christianity, and Islam. Inside these four chambers there is a flower, the flower of the *qalb*, which is the divine qualities of God. That is the second state, the flower of grace or *rahmah*. God's fragrance only exists within this inner *qalb*

Qanat: A system of underground aqueducts.

Qanat: Underground irrigation system carrying water from its source sometimes as far as 50 miles. The channel is normally about 20 feet below ground and Qanat diggers are able to alter the incline so as to take the water over low obstacles.

Qanun: Customary or administrative law in Islam, recognized by Royal decree. The growth of qanun was an inevitable development of commerce and industry and the conquest of countries whose laws were already codified like the Byzantine provinces ruled by Justinian's code. Positive law; positive law (subordinate to the Sharia) Canon of…

Qarada: A well of…

Qari: Reciter, particularly of the Qur'an.

Qasida, The: Ode; designed to praise the poet himself, his patron, or tribe.

Qasr: Which literally means to shorten is technically used to signify the Islamic rule that during one's journey it is permissible and indeed preferable, to pray only two Rak'ah in those obligatory Prayers in which a person is required to pray four ra'kahs

Qaswa: Muhammad's favorite camel

Qatlu nafsi hi: Suicide is forbidden in Islam

qawali: Muslim devotional music from South Asia

Qawm: People or nation; tribe

Qawwam: Or qayyim is a person responsible for administering or supervising the affairs of either an individual or an organization, for protecting and safeguarding them and taking care of their needs.

Qaynuqa (Banu): A Jewish tribe in Medina, allied with the Meccans. An Arabian town where the Muslims carried out their first military raid against the Quraysh

Qaysariyya: A lockup market for the sale and storage of valuable goods, fine cloth, jewelry, spices etc. Often patrolled by night watchmen.

Qibla: "The Niche of God"; in the mosque, toward which the whole Muslim world would turn in prayer, facing Mecca.

Qibla: The direction of the Ka'ba in Mecca toward which Muslims must turn during the five daily prayers and the communal prayer on Friday. As Islam spread from Arabic to vast regions in the East and the West, determining the qibla was

186

sometimes an important problem requiring mathematical calculations. The direction one faces in prayer. For Jews, the *qiblah* is Jerusalem; for Muslims, it is Mecca. Internally, it is the throne of God within the heart [*qalb*] The orientation of Muslims for salat, or ritual prayer, at first to Jerusalem, and then to Mecca.

Qisas: (*Arabic: derivative of gasas, tracking the enemy's footsteps*) The concept in Islam of equal retaliation for harm inflicted, with a provision for forgiveness, it is encapsulated in the Quran (5:49): "A life for a life, an eye for an eye/a nose for a nose, an ear for an ear/ a tooth for a tooth, and for wounds/retaliation; but whosoever forges it/ as a freewill offerings, that shall be for him/ an expiation." Equitable retribution- a fine for murder if the heirs forgive the perpetrator (see Hudud, tazeer); literally means doing with another person what he himself has done

Qitaal fee sybil Allah: Fight in the cause of Allah, a Qur'anic commandments

Qital: Fighting, killing

Qitas: Analogy, the principle in jurisprudence used to deal with new situations not mentions in the Qur'an or Sunna.

Qiyam: To stand, a position of salah prayer

Qiyama: Literally, "resurrection." The Koran refers in a number of places to yawm al qiyama, the day of resurrection. This is preceded by the destruction of all the living and followed by the day of final judgment. (A) the standing forth; the Day of Reckoning.

Qiyas: (*Arabic: to compare*):Qiyas is the method by which statements in the Quran and the Hadith are applied to situations not explicitly covered by these sources of the Islamic law. *See also ittihad.* Analogy-foundation of legal reasoning and thus fiqh; reasoning at the waist in the ritual prayer, followed by prostrations. Reasoning by analogy; legal judgments made by Islamic scholars based on the Quran, Sunnah, and the opinions of the first generation of Muslims Analogical deduction.

Qiyas: Analogy

Qiyass: Opinion of scholars; law.

Qryamah **(A):** The standing forth; the Day of Reckoning

Quba: Offering

Qubba: (Arabic "Dome"): Applied to any large domed building e.g. Dome of the Rock in Jerusalem. In the later Middle ages it came to be applied in particular to mausolea and is therefore one of the common words for the tomb.

Qubbat Al-Sakhra: Dome of the Rock, built on top of the Temple Mount in Jerusalem

Qudayd: Manat, goddess of fate

Qudrah **(A):** The power of God's grace and the qualities which control all other forces

Quds: Holy

Qudsi: Classification of a hadith that are believed to be narrated by Muhammad from God.

Saul Silas Fathi

Qur'an (also Koran): Literally, "the recitation"; the holy book of
Islam. It was revealed by Allah in Arabic. Its language
became this basis of formal and classical Arabic, written
and spoken. Revelation of the Qur'an began during the
month of Ramadan in A.D. 610, when the Prophet was in
the cave of Hira near the summit of Jabal Nur mountain.
The angel Gabriel appeared with the first revelation, the
beginning of Surah 96. the Qur'an contains laws, warnings,
descriptions of Judgment Day, heaven and hell, stories of
Biblical figures, metaphysical passages, and sacred history.
Unchanged since revelation, and considered eternal and
uncreated in its essence, the Qur'an is revered as the divine
word of Allah, and is recited in prayer. (*Arabic:
Recitation*): Muslims regard the Qur'an, which is
composed of the divine revelations received by the Prophet
Muhammad (AD 570-632) over the last twenty years of his
life from the eternal heavenly Book, *al kitab*, assessable
only to the immaculate, as the World of Allah. The Qur'an
confirmed that the law was given to Moses, the Gospel to
Jesus Christ, and the Book of Psalms to David. Jews and
Christians were called *ahl al kitab*, People of the Book.
They were subsequently taken down on palm leaves, camel
bones, or leather patches. The work of compilation,
assigned by Caliph Abu Bakr (r. AD 632-34) to the
Prophet's secretary, Muhammad Zaid ibn Thait. It was
completed before Abu Bakr's death and produced a sheaf
of separate inscribed leaves. The authorized version of the
Qur'an was not issued until AD 651 by Caliph Othmanh (r.
AD 644-56), who destroyed all other versions. It consists of
114 *suras* (chapters) of varying lengths to form a book of
some 6,616 verses. Until his migration in AD mid-622 to
Medina from Mecca, the Prophet Muhammad was under
attack by his opponent. Except for the short introductory

189

sura, the others are arranged approximately according to their length, starting with the longest. These advocate obedience to Allah in view of the forthcoming Day of Judgment. All the suras are emphatic about monotheism, urging the audience to accept no divinity except Allah. He is the one who has created the universe and maintains it, and is the most powerful and wise. Human beings, who are capable of doing good or evil, have a choice, and are responsible for their deeds as individuals and as a group. They are enjoined to heed the Quran. On the day of reckoning each person's actions will be examined and judgment delivered. He/she will either enjoy the gardens of heaven or suffer the horror of hell. the Medinese section of the Qur'an is concerned with commenting on social affairs and providing a corpus of law. It deals firstly with the external and internal security of the Islamic *umma* (community)....*qisas*. Secondly, family life is regulated. Thirdly, certain ethical and legal injunctions must be obeyed. Intoxicants, flesh of swine, games of chance and hoarding are forbidden. Pious Muslim memorize it. Often social and political gatherings begin with recitations from it. Together with the Hadith, it constitutes the Sharia. 'recitation'; 114 chapters (surahs); 6,600 verses.

Qurayzah: A Jewish tribe of Medina; Muhammad supervised their massacre after they betrayed an alliance with the Muslims Jewish tribe, enemy of Muhammad

Qurban : Externally, it is a ritual method for the slaughter of animals to purify them and make them permissible, or *halal* to eat. Inwardly, it is to sacrifice one's life to the devotion and service of God and to cut away the beastly qualities within the heart of man that cause him to want to slaughter animals

Qurbat: Closeness to God. Term is associated with Sufism

Quth : Divine analytic wisdom, the wisdom which explains; that which measures the length and breadth of the seven oceans of the *nufs*, or base desires; that which awakens all the truths which have been destroyed and buried in the ocean of maya; that which awakens true *iman* [absolute faith, certitude, and determination]; that which explains to the *hayah*, to life, the state of purity as it existed in *al-awwal*, the beginning of creation; the grace of the *dhat*, the essence of God, which awakens the *hayah* of purity and transforms it into the divine vibration. *Qutb* is also a name which has been given to Allah. He can be addressed as *Ya Qutb* or *Ya Quddus*, the Holy One. *Quddus* is His *wilayat*, His power or miracle, while *Qutb* is His action. *Wilayah* is the power of that action. Lit.: axis, axle, pole, pivot. Also, a title used for the great holy men of Islam

Ra'i: Opinion or personal judgment of faqihs in interpretating Qur'anic rules.

Ra'y: Rational opinion

Rabb al-Alamin: The Ruler of the universes.

Rabb: Has three meanings: i) Lord and Master; ii) Sustainer, provider supporter nourished and Guardian and iii) Sovereign and Ruler, He who controls and directs. God is Rabb in all the three meanings of the term. The rationale of the basic Qur'anic message serve none but God is that since God is man's Rabb-Lord, Sustainer, Provider, Nourisher-he alone should be the object of man's worship and service. Lord, Sustainer, Cherisher, Master.

Radiyallahi anhum: May Allah be pleased with them.

Radiyallahu anha: May Allah be pleased with hereditary

Rahim: Is from the root r h m which denotes mercy. In the Quran this attribute of God has been used side by side with Rahman. As such Rahim signifies God's mercy and beneficence towards His creatures. Moreover, according to several scholars, the world Rahim signifies the dimension of permanence in God's mercy. Compassionate, Ar Rahim means The Most Compassionate as in the Basmala. The One ever Compassionate.

Rahmah : God's grace; His benevolence; His wealth. All the good things that we receive from God are called His *rahmah*. That is the wealth of God's plenitude. If man can receive this, that is very good. Everything that is within God is *rahmah*, and if He were to give that grace, it would be an undiminishing, limitless wealth; mercy, compassion, the primary attribute of God and the source of the world. "merciful" is one of the personal names of God. According to scholars of the Arabic language and some commentators of the Quran, the word has the nuance of intensity regarding Divine Mercy. Thus the word does not just signify the One Who has mercy, it rather denotes the one who is exceedingly merciful, the one who is overflowing with mercy for all. The One Full of Compassion.

Rahmat al-'alamin : The mercy and compassion of all the universes; the One who gives everything to all His creations

Rahmatullah Wa Barakatuh: Mercy and blessings of Allah.

Rais: Ar., leader, President, departmental head.

Rajah: Title of Indian princes and some Far Eastern rulers.

Rajm: The practice of stoning

Raka'ah: One unit of Islamic prayer, or Salat. Each daily prayer is made up of a different number of Raka'ah; bending at the waist in the ritual prayer, followed by prostrations.

Raka'at (also **Raka'ah**): Prayer unit made up primarily of standing, bowing, prostration, and sitting; the cycles of Muslim prayer. A prayer made up of cycles of movements and words, each one of five daily prayers.

Rakaa: A portion of a Muslim prayer. The shortest prayer is made up of two Rakaas.

Rakah: Represents a unit of the Prayer and consists of bending the torso from an upright position followed by two prostrations.

Ramadan: (Ramadhan) *Islamic holy month of fasting* The Arabic root, r-m-d, refers to the heart of summer. The ninth month in the Islamic calendar, Ramadan is regarded holy in Islam because it was on the night of 26-27 Ramadan, *Lailat al kadr* (Night of Power), that the first divine revelation was made to the Prophet Muhammad. During this month the faithful are required to undertake fasting. During the month, between sunrise and sunset all adult Muslims are required to abstain from eating, drinking, smoking and conjugal relations. Among other things this helps them to develop self-control.

Ramla: Umm Habiba, Muhammad's wife

Rania: Queen of Jordan

Raqban: Cutter, saber; "the neck-cutter"

Rashidun: Sunnis consider the first four caliphs as the orthodox or rightly guided caliphs. They were Abu Bakr, Umar, Uthman and Ali. the four "rightly guided" caliphs, who were the companions and the immediate successors of the Prophet Muhammad: Abu Bakr, Umar ibn Al-Khattab, Uthman ibn Affan and Ali ibn Abi Talib. The Rightly-Guided.

Rasul (Rasul Allah): Messenger. Prophet Muhammad, the messenger of God. Allah's *Rasul* is His *dhat*, that is, the resplendence that emerged from His effulgence, shining radiantly as His Messenger. The manifestations of that resplendence discourses on the explanations of luminous wisdom which he imparts to Allah's creations. He is the one who begs for truth from Allah and intercedes with prayers [*du'a's*] for all of Allah's creations and for his followers. Therefore Allah has anointed His *Rasul* with this title: *The Messenger who is the savior for both worlds.* Lit.: the word *rasul* can be used to refer to any of Allah's apostles or messengers. A messenger, whose message comes from God Almighty in the form of a scripture to be heard, then recorded for future repetition, as a perpetual guide to correct conduct in this world, and preparation for Judgment in the next.

Rawda: Arabic garden. Used euphemistically in Spain and central Asia for tomb.

Rawis: Poets (Arabic).

Reconquista: Reconquest; Christian group who fought the Muslims and retook Spain in 1085, led by Alfonso VI. The recovery of Spanish territory, finally in 1491, by stages, following the Islamic conquest of 711.

Riba: Literally means to grow to increase. Technically it denotes the amount that a lender received from a borrower at a fixed rate in excess of the principal; Arabic for interest; interest, the charging and paying of which is forbidden by the Quran. Usury as prohibited in the Qur'an. Usury, or interest in excess of the legal rate.

Ribat: Literally a place here horse are tied. First the Barracks where fighters in the jihad lodged like the Ribat at Sousse in Tunisia. Then in Iran a caravansary in the country. Finally in Mamluk Egypt and Syria, a hospice for example that for pilgrims to Jerusalem by Qala un. Ar., Morocco, a fortified monastery; a dervish convent. Guarding Muslims from Infidels. Sufi hospice.

Rida: Satisfaction stage through which Sufi progresses in his search for God.

Riddah: Apostasy, rebellion, in which a person abandons Islam for another faith or no faith at all; renouncing one's religion.

Rifadah: Was the function of providing food to the Pilgrims and like hijabah and siqayah it was considered an important and honored function in Arabia during the Jahiliyah period

Rightly Guided Caliphs: The first four Caliphs – Abu Bakr,

Umar, Uthman, and 'Ali – who led the Islamic community before the Shia-Sunni split.

Rihla: Travel

Risalah: Literally message or letter. Used both in common parlance for mail correspondences and in religious context as divine message. report or epistle. Messenger, Divine communication. The means by which God reveals his nature, purpose and truth.

Rouzeh: Recital of the martyrdom of Husain, the Prophet's grandson, performed at religious gatherings in Iran, professional narrator.

Ruh : The soul; the light ray of God; the light of God's wisdom; *hayah* [life]. Of the six kinds of lives, the soul is the light-life, the ray of the light of *Nur* [the resplendence of Allah] which does not die. It does not disappear; it is the truth; it exists forever. That is the soul, the light-life; spirit, the divine in blowing that animate the universe, the Breath of the Merciful; spirit. The Islamic name for the soul.

Ruju: Return, coming back to normal consciousness

Ruk'u: The bowing performed during salat.

Rukn: Pillar one of the five religious duties prescribed for Muslims, Hajj, Salat, Sawm, Shahada and Zakat. means what is inevitable. One of the five pillars of Islam. (See Fard, Wajib)

Ruku : A posture in the daily formal *salah* [prayer] of Islam. A bending over from the torso, with head down and hands resting on knees; means to bend the body, to bow. This bowing is one of the acts required in Islamic Prayer. Additionally the same word denotes a certain unit in the Quran. The whole book for the sake of the convenience of the reader is divided into thirty parts and each juz consists usually of sixteen ruku

Sa'adah: Happiness

Sabb: blasphemy: insulting God *(sabb Allah)* or Muhammad (*sabb al-rasul* or *sabb al-nabi*).

Sabil: Public foundation for the provision of fresh water. The idea was probably adapted from the nyphaeum of Hellenistic and Roman towns but their recognition in Islam as pious foundations and their elaborate plumbing and decoration in the 13 and 15th centuries are far from the appearance of early Islamic sabil.

Sabirun: The patient

Sabr : Inner patience; to go within patience, to accept it, to think and reflect within it. *Sabr* is that patience deep within patience which comforts, soothes, and alleviates mental suffering *Ya Sabur* – one of the ninety-nine names of Allah. God, who in a state of limitless patience is always forgiving the faults of His created beings and continuing to protect them; patience, endurance, self restraint. Patient resolve and perseverance in the face of adversity. This quality is a sign of true faith in God.

Sadaqa: Voluntary contribution of Alms by Muslims; charity voluntary alm above the amount for zakat; voluntary charity. Voluntary almsgiving

Sadr, The: A State appointed official in Shi'ism.

Safa: A hill near the Kaaba.

Safiyya bint Huyayy: Wife of Kinana ibn Rabi; Muhammad took her as his own wife after killing Kinana. Wife of the Prophet. She was the daughter of Sheikh Huayy, leader of the Jewish-Arab Bani Nadir clan of Medina, and the widow of another great Jewish sheikh who was executed during the siege of Khaybar.

Sahaba: Companions of the Prophet. The people who accepted Islam and saw or heard him directly. Companions of Muhammad's Sahih: Sound in Isnad, a technical attribute applied to the isnad of a hadith.

Sahib: An Arabic word with a wide range of related but different meanings. These include 1) companion or associate 2) owner or possessor and 3) master or lord. Combined with other words, it is used in titles as the equivalent of Excellency, eminence, highness, etc. Passing from Arabic to Persian and from Persian to the various Muslim languages of India, it came to be the title by which gentleman, and more especially but not exclusively European gentlemen, were addressed. The *ahadith* were evaluated based on the confidence that one can have in their authenticity; a *sahih hadith* is considered sound

Sahih: Authentic

Sahn: A flat courtyard normally inside early Islamic mosques e.g. that of Ibn Tulun in Cairo. Also used however of the interior of the khanqah of Sayf al Din Bakharzi at Bukhara.

Saivam : Inner purity; in common usage it refers to vegetarianism

Saj: Adab prose; rhythmic prose.

Sajdah : In the formal prayer of Islam, [*salah*], a position of prostration on hands and knees, with forehead touching the ground

Saki: see saqi

Sakina (Shekhinah): divine "tranquility" or "peace" which descends upon a person when the Qur'an is recited.

Salaam: Peace, colloquial: greetings. Hence Islam as religion of peace

Salaat al Istikharah: Prayer for guidance is done in conjunction with two rakaahs of supererogatory prayer

Salaat I Eid: Holiday prayers.

Salaat I Jumu'ah: The gathering prayer, optional for women.

salaat: The five formal daily prayers

Salaat-I-Janazah: Funeral prayer.

Salaf (Salafi): Ancestors; the Muslims of the first generation(s). Predecessors appellation of the first generation of Muslims, Salafi: term describing the 20th century reform movement inspired by them. Early Muslims. Literally, the *predecessors*, whose acts and beliefs provided a model for later generations of Muslims. Later Muslims, inspired by the interpretative insights of these early Muslims, attempted to follow their example and developed a movement known as the Salafiyya school of thought. the forerunners, early successors to Muhammad. A conservative school of Islamic law, or jurisprudence, which advocates a return to adherence to what it sees as fundamental principles of Islam.

Salafis: Forerunners the original, pious successors of Muhammad.

Salafism: A term derived from the Arabic word for predecessors or early generations, Salafism is an austere Islamic movement that claims to be returning to the pure Islam practiced by Prophet Muhammad and the first generation of Muslims

Salafist: Follower of the pious ancestors or of original Islam, characterized by extreme rigor

Salafiya: Ideology of following the precedents of the first generation of Muslims

Salah: Any one of the daily five prayers. Literally means prayer. In Islamic parlance salah refers to the ritual which is so called because it includes praying. Salah is an obligatory act of devotion which all adult Muslims are required to perform five times a day and consists of certain specific acts such as takbir which singles the commencement of Salah and included such other acts as qiyam and ruku.

Salakis: Pious successors to Muhammad

Salam : The peace of God. Greetings! There are many meanings to the world *salam*. When we say *al-salam*, it means in God's name or in the presence of God, both of us become one without any division; both of us are in a state of unity, a state of peace; Peace, specifically, the peace conferred by God on those who accept Him, worship Him and obey Him as creator, guide and judge both of humankind and of all sentient as well as non-sentient beings.

Salat (Second Pillar of Islam): Five daily prayers; prayer in general.

Salat al Khawf: Means Prayer in the state of insecurity. For its procedure see Surah al Nisa 4:102

Salat al-Jumu'ah: Friday congregational prayer

Salat: Prayer; one of the "Five Pillars" of Islam. The daily act of worship, consisting of five prayers, addressed to God at specific times from sunrise to early evening; canonical or ritual prayer; the obligatory five daily prayers to be performed at stated times, after ablution is made.

Salawat (sing. *salah*): Prayer; usually used for the supplications asking God to bless the prophets and mankind. See also: *Salla Allah 'alayhi wa-sallam* (A)(Sing. **Salah**) prayer; usually used for the supplications asking God to bless the Prophet Muhammad. The plural form is used when asking God to bless the prophets and mankind.

Salih: Pious

Sallallahu alayhi wa sallam: "May Allah bless him and grant him peace." The expression
should be used after stating Prophet Muhammad's name. See abbreviation: *S.A.W. or S.A.W.S.* also *P.B.U.H.*

Glossary of Arabic Terms

Salsabil: a river in heaven

Sama: Listening, listening to the recitation of Qur'an or poetry, listening to music, music accomplished by ritual dancing

Samad: Eternal, absolute, Muslims believe Allah is the "eternal".

Saniyya lands: Lands belonging to the Ottoman sultan

Sanusiayyah: A movement

Saqi: Cupbearer, the one who pours the wine of love, an image derived from Qur'an 76:21, their Lord pours them pure wine.

Saqiya: The horizontal water wheel driven by a buffalo or ass generally into one or more vertical water wheels to raise water high enough for adequate pressure to be maintained. This was perhaps an Egyptian invention and was particularly popular in Islamic Egypt. The same principle was used to work oil pressed and sugar mills.

Saracen: A word of disputed etymology, used in late Greek and Latin and subsequently in the languages of Christian Europe to designate first the nomadic peoples of the desert adjoining Syria and Iraq, later the Arabs and eventually the Muslim peoples of the Mediterranean countries in general. The term is now obsolete.

Satan: In Arabic shaytan, he appears frequently in the Koran, especially in the role of tempter as for example in the final chapter (114) in which the believer is urged "to seek refuge with God from the evil of the insidious tempter, who whispers in the hearts of men." Thus, when Khomeini described the US as "the great Satan," he was not alluding to the more common accusations of imperialism, domination, exploitation and the like, but rather to the dangerous allure of the sinful Western way of life seen as a threat to the purity of the Islamic faith and order

Satraps: Local governor(s) under the Persian empire.

Saum: Fasting during the daylight hours of the month of Ramadan. Fasting. Also spelled **Siyam.**

S.A.W. (or S.A.W.S.): Sallallahu alayhi wa sallam. See *P.B.U.H.*

Sawa: Awakening, revival

Sawdah: Second wife of Muhammad who came into his household after the death of Khadijah as a thirty year old widow and a stepmother to his daughters. She had been one of the first Muslims to escape persecution by pagan Mecca and emigrate to Ethiopia. Cousin and sister-in-law of Suhayl, Chief of Amir. Married Muhammad.

Sawm (Fourth Pillar of Islam): Fasting; abstention from food and drink from dawn to sunset during the month of Ramadan.

Sayyeds: Descendants of the Prophet; also called Sharif and Shah

Sayyid: Descendant of the Prophet Muhammad

Seal of Prophecy: A title of Muhammad, considered the last prophet and messenger of Allah; also the large lump of flesh ("the size of a pigeon's egg") in the small of the back of Muhammad, interpreted as a physical sign of his prophecy.

Seerah: Biography of the Prophet Muhammad.

Sema: Refer to some of the ceremonies used by various Sufi orders; *see* sama

Semahane: House of listening where Sufis perform sama

Seveners: *see* Ismailis.

Shaab: People

Shabadah: The Muslim proclamation of faith: "I bear witness that there is no god but Al-Lah and that Muhammad is his Messenger."

Shadeed: A martyr, literally a witness

Shadhiliyyah: Sufi order (mysticism)

Shafa'I (Shafeite): Islamic school, Sunni. One of four juridical schools of Sunni Islam, prominent in Southwest Asia and East Africa

Shafi'd: School of law founded by Muhammad ibn Idris Ash-Shafi'd (d. 820). This school is dominant in Indonesia, Malaysia, and the Philippines. Along with the Hanafi and Maliki schools, it is also observed in Egypt and is followed in Central Asia and the Caucasus.

Shafii Code: *Sunni Islamic school* The Sunni [*qv*] Islamic school was named after Muhammad ibn Idris al Shafii (A.D. 767-820) The Shafii school, founded by Shafii's disciples and originating in Egypt, reached southern Arabia and from there spread along the monsoon route to East Africa and

Southeast Asia through Arab traders. Today it is particularly strong in Yemen.

Shah: The old Persian word for king, used by the monarchs of ancient Iran and revived in Islamic times. It disappeared with the dethronement of the last Shah of Iran and the abolition of the monarchy in that country in 1979. Shahanshah, "king of kings," conveys the meaning of the supreme monarch or emperor. This way of indicating hierarchic supremacy dates back ancient Iran and was retained after the advent of Islam. The Chief kadi was the kadi of kadis; the chief amir was the amir of amirs. In Turkish, the governor general of a group of provinces was called the Beylerbey, that is, the bey of beys. The title adopted by the bishops of Rome, Servus Servorum Dei, the Servant of the Servants of God, may be a distant echo of this practice.

Shahadah: Profession of faith whereby Muslim declares his acceptance of God and his Prophet, one of the rukns of Islam. The basic statement of faith "There is no God but God, Muhammad is his Prophet. To this Shias add "Ali is the friend of God." The witness, or affirmation, that there is no god but God, and that Muhammad is his last Prophet, his greatest servant, his complete messenger; the first, necessary step to become Muslims and be a member of the ummah; "bearing witness" to the oneness of God and to the prophethood of Muhammad. Also the first of the Five Pillars of Islam.

Shahbandar: Customs officer or harbor-master.

Shahid (female shaheeda): Usually translated martyr, from an Arabic verb meaning to bear witness or to testify. At the present time, it is used commonly to denote the new phenomenon of the suicide bomber. Shahid is the linguistic equivalent of the Greek word martyrs, "witness," from which our word martyr is derived. The Muslim conception of martyrdom is however, somewhat different from that of either the Jews or the Christians. The words of the Oxford English Dictionary, a martyr is one who voluntarily undergoes the penalty of death for refusing to renounce the Christian faith, one who undergoes death on behalf of any belief or cause, or through devotion to some object. In the Muslim perception, a shahid is one who gives his life fighting for the faith, in other words, in a holy war. The shahid enjoys special rewards in heaven. A word from the same root, shahada in the sense of testifying to the true faith is one of the five pillars of Islam

Shahinshah: A priest or witch-doctor claiming direct contact with a divinity.

Shaikh: Elder, head of the tribe or Sufi master; elder teacher Sufi master; lit. old man, fig. Sacred law of Islam in Arab Iraq, either an Arab tribal chieftain or a religious scholar; in Kurdish Iraq, a man of saintly descent, usually head of the religious order

Shaitan (or shaytan); plural; shayateen: An evil jinn; a devil or demon.

Shakir: Means he who acknowledges benefaction. This is the sense of the word when it is used with reference to man. When used in connection with God it denotes appreciation on God's part of man's service.

shalwar kameez: A long tunic and pants, the style of dress that is common among both men and women in the Indian subcontinent. Tunics and pants of bright colors and designs; worn by Muslim women in southeast Asia.

Sharia: (from Arabic, 'path') The law of Islam. In its widest sense the *sharia* is the way of life ('path') prescribed for Muslims, based on the Koran and the Hadith. This contains, and is sometimes identified with, *fikh* (jurisprudence), the science of the *sharia* worked out by the four orthodox schools in Sunni Islam and by Imam Jafar Sadiq (c. 700-65) and other *imams* in Shiite Islam. Although the *sharia* has no codifications in some Western law systems, the *fikh* books may be considered the equivalent of law books. Legal opinions based on *fikh* known as *fatwas* are given by scholars known as *muftis*. A religious law, believed to be divinely revealed, the *sharia* may be divided into two major categories: duties to God, which are summarized in the Five Pillars of Islam; and duties to fellow men, including penal, commercial, and family law. Pakistan announced plans to make the *sharia* the supreme law of the land in 1991 whereas in Algeria the authorities closed down the pro-*sharia* Islamic Salvation Front in early 1992. Islamic law regarding the duties of Muslims toward Allah; law distilled from the holy texts of Islam and traditional jurisprudence the body of rules guiding the life of a Muslim

Sharif: (or **Sayyid**): a descendant of Muhammad. A title accorded to the heads of prominent families entrusted with tribal or urban administration. Soon restricted to kinsmen of Muhammad and their descendants. They enjoyed special respect and Mecca was governed by Alid sharifs from the 10th century to 1924. A descendant of the Prophet's grandson Hasan by his daughter Fatima; a nobleman. A term with the general meaning noble or high born, applied particularly to descendants and kinsmen of the Prophet. In medieval, Ottoman, and early modern times, it came to be the regal title of the Amirs of Mecca until they were ousted and their realm taken over by Ibn Saud in 1925 and 1926. The title Sharif has also been used by the royal house of Morocco.

Sharr : That which is wrong, bad, or evil, as opposed to *khayr* or that which is good

Shath: Roaming or straying, whereby a mystic addresses his audience as though he were God.

Shaykh: a spiritual master, Muslim clergy

Shaykh Al-Islam: A chief justice of Islamic law appointed by the state. Religious advisor to the sultan.

Shaykh al-Juwayni: Sufi who brought the Mongols into Islam (Baghdad)

Shaytan: Literally means refractory, rebellious, and headstrong. Although this word has generally been used in the Qur'an for the satans amongst the jinn, it is also used occasionally for human beings possessing satanic characteristics; "To pull away from." Satan in Arabic. He who separates man from God.

Shazalis: Sufi Order in North Africa

shebab: Youth

Sheikh or Shaykh: An Arabic word meaning "old man." This term is frequently mispronounced. To achieve an approximately correct pronunciation, one should pronounce the first part rather like the English word "shake." And the final consonant like the ch in the Scottish Loch At a time and in a place when older men were presumed to have greater wisdom and were, therefore, entrusted with greater power, the word also acquired the connotations of leadership, dignity, and authority. Among the Bedouin Arabs, a sheikh has been since remote antiquity, and still is today, the head of the tribe. In some of the principalities of modern Arabia, it has been used as a hereditary title of rulers. Such territories are sometimes called sheikhdoms. After the advent of Islam, sheikh also came to be used as the title of a religious dignitary, especially a graduate of a theological seminary. It was also applied to the heads of religious orders and fraternities and sometimes also of craft guilds, often associated of such fraternities. The title "Sheikh al Islam" literally the old man of Islam was in medieval times conferred by consensus on eminent theologians. Under the Ottomans, it was the official title of the Chief Mufti of Istanbul, the head of the entire religious establishment of the Empire. A similar but not identical semantic development in the usage of words connoting, old age maybe also be observed in English. From the Anglo Saxon "old," we get elders and aldermen; from the Latin senex an old man, came senior, senator and senile. 'old man' – a title indicating respect. Most commonly used for learned teachers, but in Arabia also for political rulers, or simply people of importance; a tribal leader or elder, the leader of a Sufi community; term of reverence for an ordained religious leader in Islam

Sheikhdom: Literally, the domain ruled by a sheikh; here used as a shorthand for the oil exporters with the smallest populations and the largest per capita incomes.

Shia *(Arabic: Partisan): Islamic sect* Shia or Shiat means Shia/Shiat Ali, Partisans of Ali, cousin and son-in-law of the Prophet Muhammad (A.D. 570-632). They were an important part of the coalition that engineered the Abbasid revolution in A.D. 751 against the Umayyad caliphs (A.D. 661-750) The consequences were the subjugation of the Sunni caliph in Baghdad [*qv*] by a Shia king, Muizz al Dawla al Buyid, in A.D. 932, and the emergence of an Ismaili [*qv*] Shia caliphate, the Fatimids, in Cairo [*qv*] in A.D. 969. By then three branches of Shiism had crystallized: Zaidis [*qv*], Ismailis, and Imamis [*qv*]. During the Buyid hegemony in Baghdad (A.D. 932-1055) two collections of Shia Hadith [*qv*] were codified. The Shia credo consists of five basic principles and ten duties. While sharing three principles with Sunnis–monotheism, i.e., there is only one God; prophethood, which is a means of communication between God and humankind; and resurrection, i.e., the souls of dead human beings will be raised by God on their Day of Judgment and their deeds on earth judged–Shias have two more: *imamat* [*qv*] and *aadl* (justice), the just nature of Allah. Shias believe that only those in the lineage of the Prophet Muhammad–and thus of his daughter, Fatima, and her husband, Ali–can govern Muslims on behalf of Allah, and that the imams, being divinely inspired, are infallible. (In contrast, Sunnis view Islamic history essentially as a drift away from the ideal community that existed under the rule of the first four Rightly Guided caliphs: Abu Bakr, Omar, Othman and Ali). Shia emotionalism finds outlets in mourning Imams Ali (assassinated), Hassan (poisoned), and Hussein (killed in battle), and in the heartrending entreaties offered at their shrines. Unlike in the Sunni religious establishment, Shia clerics are ranked from *thiqatalislam* (trust of Islam) to *hojatalislam* (proof of Islam) to *ayatollah* (sign of Allah) to *ayatollah-ozma* (grand ayatollah). partisans or followers. Literally, "party" or "sect," specifically referring to the "party of Ali"; a Muslim who follows Ali (the cousin and fourth successor of Muhammad), who was deposed as leader of Muhammad's followers.

Shiat Ali: The Party of Ali (The Partisans of Ali); Ali's followers and army; established the Shia sect within Islam (1570).

shik: Title of respect given to a religious dignitary or to any prominent personality or elderly man

Shirk: Consists of associating anyone or anything with the Creator either in His being, or attributes, or in the exclusive rights (such as worship) that He has against His creatures. "Associating." Making others equal to God. The only unforgivable sin if a person dies while doing it. Associating any object or being with God. The one unforgivable sin of Islam; Association of partners to the divinity, idolatry. Greatest sin in Islam. Polytheism

Shukr: (pl. *shukur*): Contentment arising out of gratitude; the state within the inner patience known as *sabr*; that which is kept within the treasure chest of patience. Lit.: gratitude, thankfulness. *Ya Shakur* – one of the ninety-nine beautiful names of Allah. To have *shukr* with the help of the One who is *Ya Shakur* is true *shukr*; means thankfulness. In Islam, it is a basic religious value. Man owes thanks to God for almost an infinite number of things. He owes thanks to God for all that he possess – his life as well as all that makes his life pleasant, enjoyable and wholesome. And above all, man owes thanks to God for making available the guidance which can enable him to find his way to his salvation and felicity.

Shurah: Consultation; the duty of a leader to seek the consultation of religious experts or the people; consultation, colloquial, consultative body. Mutual consultation; an Islamic political system. A consultative council. **Majlis ash-shura:** advisory council in a Caliphate.

Siddhi (T): Magic; miracle; supernatural abilities commonly called miracles and obtained by controlling the elements

Sidrat al Muntaha: A lotus tree that marks the end of the seventh heaven, the boundary where no creation can passionate Sirah: life or biography of the Prophet Muhammad's Sirat al Mustaqim: the straight path

Sifat (A) (sing. *sifah*): The manifestations of creation; attributes; all that has come to appearance as form

Sifr: Zero (empty object), Zephyrum.

Sijjin: The register in which the people of Hell have their names written.

Silsilah: "Chain of inherited sanctity or kinship connecting the leaders of Sufi orders to their founders. Chain of tradition handed down by Sufi shaykhs to their pupils comprising the individual teachings of a particular order of dervishes.

Sin: In religion, unethical act. The term implies disobedience to a personal God, as in Judaism, Christianity, and Islam, and is not used so often in system such as Buddhism where there is no personal divinity. In ancient Israel, besides personal sin there was national sin, usually idolatry; to regain God's favor the whole people had to be purified. Ex. 32-34. Crimes of a few might also be visited on all, but punishment of the criminals could avert this. Joshua 7. Apart from original sin, Christianity and Islam have no developed idea of collective sin. As to what constitutes sin, Christian ideas differ. Some Christians divide human acts into good, indifferent, and bad; others regard all acts not positively good as necessary sinful. Thus, some may think gambling is indifferent so long as no obligation is infringed, while others consider gambling wrong as such. The theory that no act is really indifferent is common among conservative evangelical Protestants. For Christians, the effect of sin may be twofold, since a sin is at once a rebellion against the omnipotent Creator, risking punishment (even hell), as well as a cause of the interruption of grace, a motion that was popularized in the Middle Ages, notably by the Cistercians in the 12th cent. and the Franciscans in the 13th. Among Protestants it was typical of Martin Luther and John Wesley. Habitual sin is called vice. Roman Catholics are required to confess individually all mortal sins. The seven deadly, or capital, sins are pride, covetousness, lust, anger, gluttony, envy, and sloth. The sins that cry out to heaven for vengeance are willful murder (Gen. 4.10), the sin of Sodom (Gen. 18.20,21), oppression of the poor (Ex. 2.23), and defrauding the laborer of his wages (James 5.4). The sin of the angels (specifically of Satan) is pride. The opposite of sin is virtue, but in Christian practice the opposite of sin is grace, i.e., the merits of Christ's virtues given to humanity

Siqayah: Signifies the function of providing water to the pilgrims in the pilgrimage season

Sira: Biography

213

Sira'a: Combat

Sirah: The Prophet's life. Life and teachings of Muhammad

Sirat: Path

Sirat: The path or bridge over the pit of Hell that all souls must pass over after they have received their verdict from God. For those who make it over, Heaven awaits. Sinners will fall into Hell.

Sirat Al-Mustaqeem: The Straight Path

Sirr (A): The secret of Allah

Sixth Imam: Ja'afar Al-Sadiq

Siyasa: The equivalent of criminal law applied by the Mamluks in Egypt by the Ottomans and other Turkish dynasties. Although in principle accepted as compatible with the Sharia it was not based upon it and its exercise was the prerogative of the ruler not the corps of Muslim judges.

Souq (Souk): A market in Islam mostly divided up by trades lined by open booths with khans, depots, baths and masjids opening off them. It thus formed the center of the Islamic town.

Spoils of War, The: Qur'an, surah 8:41.

Subah Sadiq: True dawn

Subhan Allah: Glory be to God

Subhanahu wa-ta 'ala (A): Glory is His and exaltedness! A spontaneous outpouring of love from a believer's heart upon hearing or uttering the name Allah; expression use following written name or vocalization of Allah in Arabic

Subhanallah: Expression used by Muslims to express strong feelings of joy or relief

Subhanallah: Praise be to God

Sufi (Sufism): The Islamic form of mysticism; devotees organized into orders which carried great political weight by the eighteenth century. (Arabic "Woolen") Mystical or ascetic orders in Islam united under the authority of shaykh who draws his teachings from a chain of his predecessors. Sufism becomes apparent in Islam as early as the 8th century, but contrary either Shia or heterodox Sufis are often referred to as the poor. Sufi, Sufism: the mystics and mystical spirituality of Islam. The term may derive from the fact that the early Sufis and ascetics preferred to wear the coarse garments made of wool (Arabic, **SWF**) favored by Muhammad and his companions. member of an Islamic mystical (*sufi*) order wool (suf) coarse woolen garment.

(Arabic: sufi, derivative of suf, *wool; hence man of wool, ascetic): mystical philosophy in Islam* Subscribing to the general theory of mysticism that direct knowledge of God is attainable through intuition or insight, Sufism is based on the doctrines and methods derived from the Quran. Hassan al Basri (d. A.D. 728) was the first known sufi personality. In time, two types of Sufis emerged: ecstatic and sober. Among the latter, Abu Hamid Muhammad al Ghazali (1058-1111) was the most prominent. His work became the living document for the sufi orders/brotherhoods that sprang up soon after his death. The first sufi order was

Qadiriya. Founded by Baghdad-based Abdul Qadir al Gailani (1077-1166), it stressed piety and humanitarianism. Sufism grew rapidly between 1250 and 1500, when the caliphate was based in Cairo under Mamluk sultans (1250-1517), and when Islam penetrated central and western Africa and southern India and Southeast Asia along the land and sea routes used by Arab traders. Today sufi brotherhoods exist, overtly or covertly, in most Muslim communities. A mystical tradition that emphasizes the inner aspect of spirituality through meditation and remembrance of God. The Islamic mystic movement, whose practices center on devotion to earlier Muslims renowned for their piety and, in some cases, their supernatural powers, called *baraka* in Arabic. the guardians of tradition and spiritual Islam.

Suftajas: Similar to cashier's check.

Suhoor (Suhur): Early morning meal during Ramadan, before fasting begins. The meal taken just before the dawn prayer during Ramadan. Charges the body with a supply of energy to help it last a day of fasting.

Suhuf: Sing, signifies the materials on which something is written by extension the word denotes writing itself. Parchments.

Suhus (Soo hoof): The Islamic name for the revealed scrolls of the Prophet Abraham.

Suicide: At the present time suicide and more specifically the suicide terrorist, has come to be regarded as something characteristically and distinctively Islamic. In the past, for most of the recorded history of Islam and of Islamic states and societies, the exact opposite was true. In some civilizations, such as ancient Rome and traditional Japan, suicide is not only an acceptable choice it is even in certain situations an obligation of honor. In most Christian countries, suicide is classified as both a sin and a crime, but despite this, it was general regarded as an acceptable choice in certain situations, and suicides are not infrequent in the history of Christendom. In the Islamic world, for most of Islamic history, suicide is so rare as to be almost unknown. The classical Islamic view, as laid down and elaborated in both juristic and theological literature, is that suicide is a major sin earning eternal damnation. References to suicide in the Koran are few and indirect and they have been variously interpreted. The traditions of the Prophet however, and the whole theological and juristically tradition based on them, are unequivocal. Suicide is a major sin and however virtuous a life the one who commits it may have led, he forfeits any claim to paradise and condemns himself to hell, where, according to tradition, his punishment will consist of the eternal repetition of the act of suicide. At a certain stage, the question was posed and debated: "It is permissible in a jihad for a man to throw himself against a vastly superior enemy knowing that this will lead to certain death?" The general view was that this is permissible, because he does not die by his own hand. A case in point is the Assassins who made no attempt to escape after killing their victim, but never died by their own hands. In the modern period, new doctrine on the one hand, and new weaponry on the other, posed a new question, the lawfulness or otherwise of the suicide bomber. The extremist view, adopted and expounded in the Salafi and Wahhabi literature is that this is not only permissible, it is meritorious provided that he takes a number of enemy infidels with him. The more traditional view would be that anyone who dies by his own hand, in whatever circumstances, is guilty of the sin of suicide and thereby earns eternal damnation. For the suicide bombers of today, much rests on a point of interpretation.

Sujud: The touching of the forehead to the ground during **salat**; kneeling down, a position of salat

Sukuk: bond that generates revenue from sales, profits or leases rather than interest.

Sulh: Is derived from the Arabic word musalaha it is a look at the disposal of an Islamic commander to be different to the enemy as a respite from Military Jihad.

Sulh-E Kull: A Sufi ideal of universal peace

Sulh-i-Kul: Peace with all; Sufi saying and motto.

Sultan: Originally an Arabic noun meaning rule or power, then personalized to denote the individual who exercises power. It was already used informally in this sense in the 10th century and more formally in the 11th, when it acquired the special meaning of the independent ruler of a definite territory. From then onward, it came to denote the supreme military authority as contrasted with the supreme religious authority embodied in the caliphate. After the destruction of the Abbasid caliphate in Baghdad by the conquering Moguls in 1258 CE, it became the normal title of independent sovereignty used by Muslim rulers. A few sultans still remain, but in most Muslim countries, the title is no longer in fashion. In some, the sultans were overthrown and replaced by a variety of rulers who styled themselves "president of the republic." In others, while the monarchy was retained, the title sultan was replaced by the more Western, and therefore more prestigious, title of the king. Turk., Ar., originally he who has authority, a ruler subordinate to a caliph; later, independent ruler.

Sultanate: A territory subject to sovereign independent Muslim rule. The word 'sultan' is used in the Koran and the traditions of the Prophet Muhammad to mean 'authority'. Mahmud of Ghazna was the first Muslim ruler to be addressed as sultan by his contemporaries. The term thereafter became a general title for the effective holders of power, sch as the Seljuk or Mameluke dynasties, though it was also used as a mark of respect under the Ottomans for princes and princesses of the imperial house The term 'sultanate' was also used of a number of virtually independent centers of Muslim power, such as the sultanate of Delhi (1206-1526), the predecessor of the Mogul empire in India, and the Sulu sultanate, a trading empire in the southern Philippines, which flourished between the 16th and 19th centuries.

Suluk: Wayfaring, traveling on the path to God

Sumaiyah bint Khabbab: The first Muslim woman to be murdered for her faith; stabbed by Abu Jahl.

Sunna: *(Arabic: custom, path, practice of Islam):* In the pre-Islamic society of Arabia the term *sunna* applied to social practices based on ancestral precedents. After the rise of Islam under the Prophet Muhammad (A.D. 570-632), early converts took their cue either from the behavior of the Prophet's companions or the residents of Medina, the capital of the Islamic realm. Though the Prophet Muhammad was an exemplar for Muslims, it was not until the eminent jurist Muhammad ibn Idris al Shafii (A.D. 767-820) had ruled that all legal decisions not stemming directly from the Quran must be based on a tradition going back to the Prophet Muhammad himself that a serious effort was made to compile the Prophet's sayings and doings. The *sunna* was then employed in the exposition of the Quran and in *fiqh* (Islamic jurisprudence). Literally the path following the example of Muhammad set out in the Quran and hadith, refers to the majority Muslims denomination. The pattern of God in ordering the Creation and function of the material world; the exemplary conduct of the Prophet Muhammad, conveyed in reports of his deeds, dicta and endorsements (Hadith); the necessary companion and complement to the Qur'an for many Muslims.

Sunnat: An act of which the Prophet performed, not required but carried much reward.

Sunni (Sunnis): One who follows the Sunna, the precept and practice of the Prophet and of the early leaders of Islam, as recorded by tradition. They now form the majority in most Muslim communities and control most Muslim states with the notable exception of Iran. The Christian, originally platonic, term orthodox, "correct belief," is sometimes used to designate the Sunni version of Islam. This is a misleading analogy. "mainstream would be a better description. Sunni Islam, like Rabbinic Judaism is more concerned with correct practice than with correct belief. Orthodox Islam, basing its teaching upon the Koran and its interpretation, hadith traditions reputably associated with Muhammad himself and the teaching of the four orthodox schools of law. person who follows the teachings of Prophet Muhammad. Followers of Omar as the successor of Muhammad.

(Persian: derivative of Ahl al sunna; *Arabic; People of the path [of the Prophet Muhammad]): Islamic sect* The majority of the elites and people in the Muslim world; the major "orthodox" division of Islam. Sunnis are the leading sect within Islam. They regard the first four caliphs–Abu Bakr, Omar, Othman, and Ali (r. A.D. 656-61)–"Rightly Guided." They belong to one of the four schools of jurisprudence–Hanafi, Maliki, Shafii, and Hanbali-and accept the six "authentic books" of al Hadith, the first of which was compiled by Muhammad al Bukhari (d. A.D. 870). Sunnis and Shias also differ on the organization of religion and religious activities. Sunnis regard religious activities as the exclusive domain of the (Muslim) state. The Sunni ethos, too, is different from the Shia. There is no emotional outlet for mourning the martyrdom of early Islamic leaders, as in the Ashura celebrations of Shias. Sunni clerics are not given the religious titles of their Shia counterparts. Those Muslims who believe that succession after Muhammad was to be decided by the community of believers and not by divine authority or prophetic appointment; they accept the history of the first hijri century and the authority it conferred on the Righteous Caliphs; they acknowledge Ali as the Fourth Caliph but not as the First Imam. Their successors are the Umayyad, then the Abbasid Caliphs.

Sunnism: Doctrine of the majority of the world's Muslims, which follows the example of the Prophet and legal tradition of the majority of the community.

Sura Ikhlas: The "Verse of Sincerity." It proclaims the unity or absoluteness of the Divine Essence.

Surah: Form or shape, such as the form of man; the Quran is composed of 114 suras. Chapter of the Qur'an. Fence.

Surat al-Adam : Form of Adam

Surat al-insan: The inner form of man. The inner form of man is the Qur'an and is linked together by the twenty-eight letters. The form, this *surah*, is the *Umm al-Qur'ani*, the source of the Qur'an. It is the Qur'an in which the revelations of Allah are revealed. The sounds in the Qur'an which resonate through wisdom, the Messenger of Allah, Prophet Muhammad, the angels and heavenly beings – all are made to exist in this body as secrets

Surat: Form, the form in which God created Adam, the outward appearance of a thing, contrasted with ma na

Suwayqa: Market

Ta'alaa: Almighty

Ta Allah: Deformity, theomorphic, becoming qualified by the attributes of God

Ta widh: The invocation of God's mercy from the forces of evil, specifically the wiles or insinuations of the devil.

Ta wil: Allegorical interpretation of the Quran, often imparting new meaning that goes beyond common sense commentaries and also explaining verses or letters with an ambiguous meaning.

Ta'f: The city of Al-Lat (The Goddess). A city south of Mecca that initially rejected Muhammad and was later conquered by the Muslims

Ta'ifa: Organization of a Sufi order, as distinct from its spiritual path.

Ta'widh: The invocation of God's mercy and protection from the forces of evil, specifically the wiles or insinuations of the devil.

Ta'wil: Esoteric or allegorical interpretation of the Quran, predominant among Shi'ites; the symbolic, mystical interpretation of the Koran advocated by such esoteric sects of the Ismailis. Allegorical interpretation of the Qur'an, often imparting new meaning that goes beyond common-sense commentaries and also explaining verses or letters with an ambiguous meaning. To take something back to its origin.

Ta'ziyah: Passion play held each year in Shi'i communities to commemorate the death of Husyan ibn Ali

Taba'in: Followed of the Sahabah

Tabi: A successor of the Prophet's companions

Tabiun: Successors are those who benefited and derived their knowledge from the Companions of the Prophet.

Tafakkur: Reflection, meditation, a Sufi practice

Tafsir: Commentary on the meaning of the Quran, mostly confined to verses with an evident and common sense message; commentary, explanation or exegesis of the Quran

Taghut(taghout): Literally denotes the one who exceeds his legitimate limits. In Qur'anic terminology it refers to the creature who exceeds the limits of his creatureliness and abrogates to himself godhead and lordship. In the negative scale of values, the first stage of man's error is fisq. The second stage is that of kufr. The last stage is that man not only rebels against God but also imposes his rebellious will on others. All those who reach this stage are taghout. literally denotes the one who exceeds his legitimate limits. In Qur'an terminology it refers to the creature who exceeds the limits of his creatureliness and arrogates to himself godhead and lordship. Originally Aramaic meaning false God

Tahajjud: Is the prayer offered in the last quarter of the night at any time before the commencement of the time of Fajr prayer. It is recommender rather than an obligatory prayer.

Taharah: Purity or cleanliness Purification from ritual impurities by means of wudu or ghusl

Tahir: Pure and ritually cleaned

Tahkim: Arbitration

Tahlil: Prayer la ilaha illa Allah, there is no deity but God, particularly used in Sufi Rituals. Uttering the formula of faith.

Tahnik: Is an Islamic ceremony of touching the lips of a new born baby with honey

Tahrif: Corruption, forgery.

Tahrik: Movement

Taif: The city of al-Lat and center of paganism. Muhammad's enemies Surrender in Jan 631

Taiyyat: Natural philosophy

Tajdid: To purify and reform society in order to move it toward greater equity and justice. Renewal of the Islamic religion. This process is viewed by modern Islamists as essential to retaining the religion's relevance to contemporary society.

Tajdif: Blasphemy

Tajweed: Pronunciation during recitation of the Qur'an; a special manner of reciting the Qur'an according to prescribed rules of pronunciation ad intonation

Takaful: Based on sharia Islamic law it if form of mutual insurance

Takbir: Saying: *"Allah Akbar"*; a proclamation of the greatness of Allah, a Muslim invocation; saying **"Allahu akbar,"** literally "God is greater," often used as a signal of commendation.

Takfir: Declaration of individual or group of previously considered Muslim as kaffir. Excommunication, to pronounce someone as an infidel. imputation of impiety, excommunication. The act of denouncing one who claims to be a Muslim as a Kafir and thus in effect to accuse him of the capital crime of apostasy. In Earlier times, Takfir was comparatively rare and was only pronounced by a properly constituted religious authority. More recently, the term is used by radical and violent Islamic sects to condemn and silence their more moderate critics and opponents.

Takfir Wal-Hijra: Repentance and holy flight.

Takhrij: The science of hadith extraction and authentication, including validation of chains of transmitters of a hadith by this science's scholars and grading hadith validity.

Talaq: Declaration of divorce by the husband according to the Shari'a; means repudiation of marriage

Talbiya: A phrase declared by the pilgrims to Mecca: "Here I am, God, at thy service."

Talfiq: Synthesis of rulings of different schools of law

Talhah: Aisha's kinsman

Talib: Student, often a pupil at an Islamic school or *madrasa*.

Tamaninat: to be motionless

Tanzimat: Administrative decrees, reforms instituted by the nineteenth century Ottoman sultans; reorganization; the reforms undertaken in the Ottoman Empire during the mid-nineteenth century, under West European influence. Regulations. Reorganization.

Taqdir: Fate predestination

Taqdis: Has two meanings 1) to celebrate and proclaim holiness; 2) to purify

Taqiyya: Dissimulation of one's beliefs in the face of danger, especially among Shi'ites; the mostly Shia principle that one is allowed to hide one's true beliefs in certain circumstances. Usually translated dissimulation, the disguising of one's true feelings or beliefs. This is based on a verse in the Koran that threatens a mighty punishment for those who, after professing faith in God, revert to unbelief. This verse does, however, make an exception for those who do so under compulsion, their heart remaining firm in faith. An early commentator explains: "If anyone is compelled and professes unbelief with his tongue, while his heart contradicts him, in order to escape his enemies, no blame falls on him, because God takes His servants as their hearts believe." The doctrine of Taqiyya, while not formally rejected by the Sunnis, was much of more important in Shi'a doctrine and practice, understandably, since at most times and in most places the Shi'a were the minority, and subject to the domination of the Sunni majority or in any case of Sunni rulers. Originally referring only to matters of religious belief and practice, the notion of taqiyya has been given a much wider extension today. A classical example cited by the jurists is a certain Ammar ibn Yasir, an early convert to Islam in Mecca who was severely tortured because of his beliefs and is said to have made some partial recantation. Later he escaped to Ethiopia and from there rejoined the Prophet in Medina, where he played an active role in the early Islamic state. The name Abu Ammar "Father of Ammar" sometimes used by the late Yasir Arafat, was an evocation of this early Islamic hero.

Taqlid *(Arabic: to hang around the neck):* Initially a practice of designing a sacrificial animal with a sign around its neck, but later extended to designating a public official with a badge or chain around his neck. Following or imitating a religious authority. (Can have favorable or unfavorable connotations according to context.) Imitation or emulation. Imitation or the basing of legal decisions on the existing judgments of the four Sunni madhhabs. To follow the scholarly opinion of one of the four Imams of Islamic jurisprudence

Taqwa: (Arabic) God-consciousness; righteousness, goodness, Piety. The conscious awareness that God is watching you; the mostly Shia principle that one is allowed to hide ones true belief; to approach God with reverence and piety. Awareness. Humans relationship to God, piety and reverence, not fear.

Tarahan, singhan, **and** *suran* : The three sons of maya or illusion. *Tarahan* is the trench or the pathway for the sexual act, the birth canal or vagina. *Singhan* is the arrogance present at the moment when the semen is ejaculated (karma). It is the quality of the lion. *Suran* is the illusory images of the mind enjoyed at the moment of ejaculation. It is all the qualities and energies of the mind

Taraweeh: An evening prayer in a mosque, after a day of fasting.

taraweeh: The special evening prayers observed during Ramadan; extra prayers in Ramadan after the Isha prayer.

Tarbiyyah: Education, cultivation or growth.

tarbiyyah: The religious upbringing of children

Tariqah: a Muslim religious order, particularly a Sufi order

Tariqa: Path, way; the path we need to walk in our personal and social lives in order to live in conformity with reality. Sufi; "ways", paths Islamic mystical order (Sufi)

Tarkib: The study of Arabic grammar issued from the Quran

Tartil: Slow, meditative recitation of Quran

Tasanwuf: Islamic mysticism

tasaqquf: Sufi way or path

Tasawwaf: Islamic mysticism, purification of self.

Tasawwuf: Mysticism, Sufism. Spirituality. Islamic esotericism.

Tasbih : The glorification of God; has two meanings: 1) to proclaim the glory of God 2) to exert earnestly and energetically in the service of God. Uttering the formula Subhan Allah Glory be to Allah

Tasbih (Musbaha): To glorify (God)

Tasfir: Qur'anic scholarship; exegesis. Scholarly commentary

Tashahhud: Literally testimony is a declaration of the Muslims faith towards the end of the Prayers, immediately after the recitation of Tahiyah, while sitting with the first finger of the right hand extended as a witness to the unity of God.

Tashahhud: Words of supplication and praise (the shahadah).

Tashkil: Vocalization of Arabic text by means of diacritical marks

Tasleem: Salutation of peace: "Peace and God mercy be with you" (Arabic)

Taslim: Salutation at the end of prayer

Tassawwuf: Sufi way or path.

Tatbeer: Shia Ashura ceremony of self-flagellation by hitting head with sword (See zinjeer)

Tauhid (Tauwheed): "Oneness or monotheism." A term used to emphasis the unitary nature of God. Central unity of God, monotheism, God's sovereignty over the universe; monotheism, the unity of Allah. Unity of God

Taurat (Tawrah): The Arabic name for the Torah of Moses.

Tawaf: Circumambulating the Babah during Hajj. Ritual circumambulation of the Ka'ba by a pilgrim during the Hajj or Umra. Seven ritual circumambulations of the Shrine of Ka'aba, following the direction of sun

Tawakkul 'ala Allah (A): Absolute trust and surrender; handing over to God the entire responsibility for everything. Lit.: "Trust in Allah"

Tawakul: Total reliance on Allah

Tawassul: Asking Allah Almighty through the medium and intercession of another person

Tawba: "Repentance." Asking forgiveness from God for a sin.

Tawbah: "Repentance." Asking forgiveness from God for a sin. basically denotes 'to come back, to turn towards someone' **Tawbah** on the part of man signifies that he has given up his disobedience and has returned to submission and obedience to God. The same word used in respect of God means that He has mercifully turned to His repentant servant so that the latter has once more become an object of His compassionate attention.

Tawha: Repentance, turning toward God as a result of his turning toward you.

Tawheed: Islamic monotheism; belief in the oneness of God. (A): The affirmation of the unity of Allah, the principal tenet of Islam. (Arabic) unity. This refers to the divine unity of God and also to the integration required of each Muslim, who strives to surrender wholly to God. Declaring oneness, asserting the unity of God, the first principle of Islamic faith; making one. The divine unity, which Muslims seek to imitate in their personal and social lives by integrating their instructions and priorities, and by recognizing the overall sovereignty of God. The theory of Allah's overriding supremacy and the secondary importance of worldly authority.

Tawil: Carrying back

Tawrah: The revelation given to Moses; the Torah

Tawrat: The Torah is revealed to Moses

Tawwaf: Performed around the Qa'aba

Tawwaf: Seven ritual circumambulations of the Qa'aba Shrine following the direction of the sun.

Tayammum: Literally means to intend to do a thing. As an Islamic legal term it refers to wiping one's hands and face with clean earth as a substitution for ablution when water cannot be obtained.

Tayamoon: Dry ablution, using clean sand or dust on the hands and face.

Tayyib: All that is good as regards things, deeds, beliefs, persons, food meaning pure.

Tazaqqa: The process of refinement.

Tazeer: Discretionary punishment. A sentence or punishment whose measure is not fixed by the Shari'ah. (See hudud, qisas)

Tazkiyah: Purification of the Soul

Tekka: Sufi gathering place or lodge. A Sufi center.

Tekkes (Turk): Sufi centers in Turkish speaking areas.

Tharid: Dish

Thawab: Denotes recompense and reward. A major thrust of Islamic teachings is that man should be concerned with the ultimate recompense that he will receive for his deeds. Some of these good or bad deeds might be recompensed in some measure in the present world. However, what is of basic importance is the Next World where the righteous will enjoy lasting bliss and the wicked will suffer lasting punishment; Reward for good deeds that is tallied on Qiyamah

The Asma al-Husna: Are the ninety-nine beautiful names of His duties. They were revealed to Prophet Muhammad in the Qur'an, and the explained them to his followers. This is a vast **hahr al-dawlah,** a very deep ocean of His grace and His limitless, infinite, and undiminishing wealth. If we go on cutting one of these ninety-nine **wilayat** over and over again, taking one piece at a time, we will see ninety-nine particles revolving one around the other without touching. This applies to each one of the ninety-nine **wilayat**. This is the **Asma al-husna**. As we go on cutting, we lose ourselves in that. We die within that. How can we ever hope to reach and end of the ninety-nine? If we receive only one drop of that, it will be more than sufficient for us. The person who has touched the smallest, tiniest drop becomes a good one. These are merely His powers. If you go on cutting just one of His powers, it is so powerful that it will draw you in. That power will swallow you up, and you become the power [**wilayah**]. Then you come to the stage at which you can lose yourself within Allah; you can disappear within Allah.

The Legend of Jihad: Islamic Holy War and the Fate of Non-Muslims

Theology: The study of God and of His relationship to the universe.

Thobe: One-piece, long-sleeved robe.

Thuluth: Islamic script; calligraphy.

Tijaniyya: A Sufi order. A dervish fraternity of worldwide membership, Tijaniyya dervishes – a strict **tariqa (q.v.)** principally in Ghana, Guinea and Senegal.

Tilawa: Ritual recitation of passages of the Quran.

Tiraz: State factories of fine cloth. They were most probably monopolies because they wove fabrics bearing the sovereign's name whih were then used for robes of honor essentially official garments.

Turath: Cultural heritage

Twelfth Imam: Shiite, named Muhammad; disappeared into a cave in 878, he will return one day before the end of the world (as a messiah), as the "Mahdi", "the Expected One" (Iran).

Twelver Shias: The predominant category among Shias, Twelvers or Twelver Shias are so called because they believe in twelve *imams*: Ali, Hassan, Hussein, Zain al Abidin, Muhammad al Baqir, Jaafar al Sadiq, Musa al Kazem, Ali al Rida/Reza, Muhammad al Taqi Javad, Ali al Naqi, Hassan al Askari, and Muhammad al Qasim. They believe that Muhammad al Qasim, the infant son of the eleventh imam, went into occultation in Samarra, Iraq, in A.D. 873, leaving behind four special assistants. As the last of them failed to name a successor, the line of divinely inspired imams became extinct in A.D. 940.

Twelvers: Twelver Shias. The largest branch of Shiite Islam. They believe that the twelfth imam, (successor to 'Ali in Shia belief) was taken by Allah and will return as a messiah figure to lead Shiite Muslims at Judgment Day.

Ubudiyah: worship

Udhiyah: sacrifice

Ulama/ulema: *(Arabic: pl. of alim, possessor of* ilm, *knowledge):* Ulama is the term used collectively for religious-legal scholars of Islam. Since *ilm* in Islam means knowledge of the Quran and the *sunna*, the ulama are theologians and canonists. They are the ultimate authority on the issues of law and theology, personifying the right of Muslims to

234

govern themselves. The custodians of ilm or knowledge who transmit it from generation to generation as teachers and jurists within the ummah. (plural of **alim**): learned men, Islamic scholars. Ar., literally, 'the knowledgeable persons', scholars of Islamic religious subjects. Essentially scholars who had to traditional madrasa education in the Koran and its exegesis, tradition, and canon law. Such scholars were appointed to the judiciary or other posts in the administration and came to form a class of urban notables, the ahl al Qalam. those learned in Islamic law. The leaders of Islamic society, including teachers, Imams, and judges. The custodians of 'ilm, or knowledge, who transmit it from generation to generation as teachers and jurists within the ummah. The established body of religious scholars. Their thoughts and writings are often closely tied to the requirements of incumbent political authorities in need of religious sanction for political acts.

Umayya: A powerful clan that controlled Mecca and opposed Muhammad's prophethood. Later embraced Islam and established a dynasty in Syria.

Umm al kitab: The Meta Book of all Divine Revelation, preceding the Qur'an 'an and finalized in the Qur'an, it included the Torah for Jews and the Injil, or Gospel for Christians as well as other scriptures.

Umm al-Qur'an (A): The 'source' or 'mother' of the Qur'an. It is used commonly to refer to the *Surat al-Fatihah,* or the opening chapter of the Qur'an. It is said that within the 124 letters of the *Surat al-Fatihah* is contained the meaning of the entire Qur'an. It is often used to denote the eternal source of all the revelations to all of the prophets and is also known as the *Umm al*-Kitah [the mother, or source of the book]. This is a divine, indestructible tablet to which all is recorded. This is the silent Qur'an which exists as a mystery within the heart [*qalb*] of each person.

Umm: *(Arabic: mother):* It is customary among many Arabs to call a married woman the "umm" of her first-born son.

umma: A derivative of either the Arabic umm, meaning mother or source; or a loan-word from Hebrew *umma* or Aramaic *ummtha; umma* appears many times in the Quran, always alluding to ethnic, linguistic, or religious groups who were part of Allah's plan of salvation. In modern times the *umma*, now meaning the worldwide Islamic community On the other hand, the annual hajj is a dramatic illustration of the existence of umma. An Arabic word usually denoting a religious community. In modern usage, it is also used to translate the term nation, as for example in the Arabic name of the United Nations. When one speaks of "the Umma" without specific qualification or designation, it is usually understood to mean the global Muslim community as a whole. The global community of Muslims, which transcends nationality and nation-states and links all Muslims into a single community.

Ummi (A): One who is unlearned, illiterate. A title given to Muhammad and found in *Surah VIII* of the Holy Qur'an; signifies the 'unlettered'. It is also used to refer to those who do not possess Divine revelation.

Ummi Prophet: The Unaltered Prophet; the prophet to the Gentiles

Ummul Mu'minin: Mother of the Believers (reference to Aisha).

Umrah: Lesser pilgrimage to Makka which can be performed at any time of the year. Pilgrimage out of due season to Mecca and Medina. This was always a pious work, but it was insufficient to satisfy the requirement that every male adult Muslims should if humanly possible make the pilgrimage one in his lifetime. Short hajj; *small pilgrimage to Mecca. Umra* involves the central ceremonies of the *hajj* for Muslims: circumambulating the Kaaba in Mecca and striding quickly between the Safa and Marwa hillocks. The lesser **hajj,** or pilgrimage to Mecca performed at any time of the year. (Minor Pilgrimage) is an Islamic rite and consists of Pilgrimage to the Ka'bah. It consists essentially of **Ihram** (q.v.), **tawaf** (i.e. circumambulation) around the Ka'bah (seven times), and **sa'y** (i.e. running) between Safa and Marwah (seven times). It is called minor **hajj** since it need not be performed at a particular time of the year and its performance requires fewer rituals than the **Hajj** proper. the ritual circumambulations around the Kabah **(q.v.).**

Uqubat: the branch of sharia that deals with punishment

Urf: Custom of a given society leading to change the fiqh. Customary law, which was often accepted in areas where the ruling madhhab was not that of the ruled as in Egypt under the Mamluks where direct application of the sharia would have led to conflicts of interest. Social ethos.

Ushr: A tithe on agricultural produce.

Usul al Fiqh: Roots or foundations of jurisprudence. In the Sunni madhhabs they comprise, the Quran the Sunna, ijma and qiyas. The study of the origins and practice of Islamic jurisprudence; Principles, origins

Usul al-Hadith: Science of hadith

Usul: Roots, principles, of the Sha'ria.

Usuliyyah: Fundamentalism

Utba ibn Rab'ia of Abd Shams: Brother of Shayba

vali: Guardianship; governor of a province (*vilayet* (Turkish))

Verse of the Rajm: ...Stoning...

Vilayat-I-Faqih: Guardianship or government by an expert in
Islamic law, the office commands enormous prestige
among Shias, for whom there can only be one Faqih at any
given time. (*Persian: Rule of the Religious Jurisprudent*):
Islamic doctrine This doctrine, developed by Ayatollah
Ruhollah Khomeini in his book *Hukumas-e Islam: Vilayet-
e Faqih (Persian: Islamic government: Rule of the Faqih)*
(1971), specified that an Islamic regime required an Islamic
ruler who is thoroughly conversant with the ruler Sharia
and is just in its application: a Just Faqih. After the
establishment of the Islamic Republic of Iran in April 1979,
the Vilayer-e Faqih doctrine became the backbone of the
Islamic constitution adopted in December 1979.

Vizier: (Arabic *wazir*) A leading court official of a traditional
Islamic regime. Viziers were frequently the power behind
nominal rulers. At times the office became hereditary,
under the early Abbasids falling into the hands of the
Barmakids and under the Ottomans in the late 17th century
held by the Koprolu family. From the Arabic wazir,
probably of Persian origin, denoting a high officer of the
state under various Muslim regimes. In its earliest

occurrences, it describes the chief executive and head of chancery of the administration under the caliphs. Under later Muslim dynasties, the office and with it the title, underwent several changes. In the Ottoman state, the vizierate initially included high military command. There were several viziers, the first or chief vizier being the Vizier A'zam or Sadr Azam, known in Europe as the Grand Vizier. He was the supreme head of the Ottoman administration for civil and military matters alike and was responsible for all aspects of government under the supreme authority of the sultan. The office of the Grand Vizier came to be known as the Bab'I Ali, commonly translated "sublime Porte." During the 19th century the Grand Vizier gradually dwindled into a Prime Minister and his office ended with the Ottoman Empire from Turk., Ar., **wazir,** a minister, officer of state, head of administration. The principal minister of the Abbasid caliphs in charge of the chancery and later of the other administrative offices of state. Although under the Seljuks the Mongols and the Ottomans viziers were often the rulers de facto deputies initially even the Barmecides at Baghdad had very little independence and were essentially subject to the caliph's every whim. a high official serving a Muslim ruler.

wa: And or by

Waaf: *see* **awqaf.** Religious endowment, generally landed property

Waby: Refers to Revelation which consists of communicating God's Messages to a Prophet or Messenger of God. The highest form of revelation is the Qur'an of which even the words are from God.

Wadi I Qura: Oasis in Arabia

Wadi: Defined by the dictionary as "a ravine or gully that occasionally turns into a water course." This derives from the Arabic wadi, with the broader meaning of a river valley in which, depending on the weather, there may or may not be a river. The term is used equally of such mighty rivers as the Nile and the Euphrates and of the normally dry water courses of the Arabian Peninsula. On maps of North Africa, the term appears in the form owed, a French transcription of the North African dialectal pronunciation of Wadi

Wafat: Death

wahadat: Unity

Wahdat al wujud: Oneness of Being, the assertion that there is only one true being that of God, a doctrine that is famously but misleading attributed to Ibn Arabi; unity of being

Wahdat al-Wujud: Unity of Being, monism (Sufi)

Wahhabi: Sect dominant in Saudi Arabia and Qatar. Founded by Muhammad Ibn abd Al-Wahhab (1703-87). Wahhabi, said to be followers of the Hanbali school, see themselves as belonging to no school, just as the first generations of Muslims did not follow schools of jurisprudence. followers of Muhammad Ibn Abdul-Wahhab, the eighteenth-century Arabian reformer.

Wahhabism and Wahhabis: sect dominant in Saudi Arabia and Qatar. Founded by Muhammad Ibn abd Al-Wahhab (1703-87). Wahhabi, said to be followers of the Hanbali school, see themselves as belonging to no school, just as the first generations of Muslims did not follow schools of jurisprudence. followers of Muhammad Ibn Abdul-Wahhab, the eighteenth-century Arabian reformer. *Islamic sect* Wahhabism is an Islamic doctrine developed by Muhammad ibn Abdul Wahhab (1703-87), a native of Najd, a bastion of Hanbalis. Unlike Hanbali practices, Abdul Wahhab made attendance at public prayer obligatory and forbade minarets in the building of mosques. Regarding themselves to be true believers, Wahhabis launched a jihad against all others—whom they described as apostates. This led the Ottoman sultan to order the governor of Egypt, Muhammad Ali, to quell the movement. The result was the defeat and execution of Abdullah ibn Saud (r. 1814-18) The power of the Wahhabi House of Saud waxed and waned until 1881, when it was expelled from the Riyadh region. They labeled any deviation from the Sharia as innovation and therefore un-Islamic. The final authority lies with the head of the Supreme Religious Council in Saudi Arabia. It has adherents in Central Asia, Afghanistan, Pakistan, and India. Doctrine of the disciples of ibn Abd al Wahhab, puritan preacher whose influence still dominates Saudi Islam

Wahn: Love of this life and hatred of death

Wahy : Revelation; inspiration from God; the inspired word of God revealed to a prophet; the commandments or words of God. *Wahys*, or revelations, have come to Adam, Moses, and various other prophets, but most of all to Prophet Muhammad. Muhammad received 6,666 revelations. The histories of each of the prophets were contained within the revelations given to Prophet Muhammad Inspiration or revelation of the Quran; refers to Revelation which consists of communicating God's Messages to a Prophet or

Messenger of God. The highest form of revelation is the Quran of which even the words are from God

Wajd: Ecstasy finding the Being of God

Wajib: Obligatory and mandatory see far

Walaikum Salaam: "And unto you be peace." Used as a response in greeting or bidding farewell.

Walayah: Denotes the relationship of kinship, support, succor, protection, friendship, and guardianship. It signifies also the relationship of mutual support between the Islamic state and its citizens, and between the citizens themselves. For details see **Surah** 8, n. 50.

Wali: Mediator; saint to whom God has granted special knowledge and Divine Wisdom; a "friend of God," a holy person or saint; friend, protector, guardian, supporter, helper.

Wali: Guardian, protector, including a father, brother or uncle of a bride.

Walima: Islamic wedding dinner. The wedding reception after a marriage ceremony; the wedding banquet or celebration.

Waqf *(Arabic: prevent):* In Islamic Law, *waqf,* the term popularly used for a religious trust mean "prevent a thing from becoming the property of a third person." The waqfs, often administered by public officials, ameliorated poverty and advanced further education. the central administration of waqfs in Egypt, begun in 1851, was formalized with a ministry in 1913. Following the 1979 Islamic revolution, this code was abrogated. (lit) prevent; (fig) religious endowment. A technical term, signifies the appropriation or dedication of property to charitable uses and to the service of God. It is an endowment the object of which must be of a perpetual nature so that the property so endowed may not be sold or transferred. A pious endowment in mortmain.

Waqfiyya: Legally attested document specifying the constitution of a pious foundation, its physical limits and its endowments in detail. Since Waqf revenues were tax free, special departments of state were set up to register property and income and contained copies of all current waqfiyyas.

Waqt **(A):** Time of prayer. In the religion of Islam there are five specified *waqts*, or times of prayer, each day. But truly, there is only one *waqt*. That is the prayer that never ends, where one is in direct communication with God and one is merged in God

Warith: Inheritors

Warraq: traditional scribe, publisher, printer, notary and book copier

Was: And or by

Wasat: The middle way justly balanced, avoiding extremes, moderation

Waseelah: The means by which one achieves nearness to Allah

Wasi: Each wasi was followed by a succession of seven imams.

Watan: Homeland or nation; Homeland or nation a concept borrowed from Western nationalism. Nation or fatherland.

In modern Arabic, usually the individual Arab state, as opposed to the greater Arab nation (**qaum**).

Waynuqah: A Jewish tribe in Medina

Wazir (Vizier): Chief executive officer to the caliph.

Wazir (Vizier): The head of the bureaucracy, the "Diwan"; his principle function was to raise money and oversee the bureaucracy.

Well of Raji: Near Mecca

Well of Usfan: ±25 miles north of Mecca

Wilayah: (Pl. **wilayat**) God's power; that which has been revealed and manifested through God's actions; the miraculous names and actions of God. See also: **Asma Al-Husna**.

Wird: Private prayer in addition to the salat.

Witr: A voluntary, optional night prayer of odd numbers; means odd number Witr Rak'ahs are odd numbers of rak'ahs such as 1, 3, 5 etc. Usually 1 or 3 which are said after the last prayer at night

Wudu: Refers to the ablution made before performing the prescribed Prayers. It requires washing (1) the face from the top of the forehead to the chin and as far as each ear; (2) the hands and arms up to the elbow; (3) wiping with wet hands a part of the head; and (4) washing the feet to the ankle. Ablution for ritual purification from minor impurities before salat. Ablution, prescribed washing done before saying prayers. Ablutions made before *salat,* the Islamic ritual prayer. Ritual purity.

Wujud: Being, existence, the Being of God other than which there is no true being

Ya Allah: O God

Ya Rasool Allah: O, Messenger of God!. Term used by companions when interacting with Prophet Mohammad.

Ya Sabur: One of the ninety-nine names of Allah. God, who in a state of limitless patience is always forgiving the faults of His created beings and continuing to protect them.

Ya Shakur: One of the ninety-nine beautiful names of Allah. To have **shukr** with the help of the One who is **Ya Shakur** is true **shukr.**

Yahiya: John the Baptist

Yahudi: The Arabic term for a Jew.

Yajooj-wa-Majooj: Gog and Magog

Yajuj: Gog (Bible)

Yaqin: Certainly that which is certain

Yarhamukallah: Arabic for "May Allah bless you"

Yasawi's: A Sufi order named for the 12th century saint of Turkestan, Ahmad Yasawi, the first major Sufi to appear in the central Asian heartland

Ya-Sin: Muslim memorial to the dead

Yathrib: Ancient name of the city of Medina; name changed to

Medina after Muhammad relocated there. Medina, north of Mecca

Yaum al Deen: Day of reckoning

Yaum al Ghadab: Day of rage

Yawm ul Qiyamah: Day of resurrection.

Year of Sadness, The: The year when Muhammad's wife Khadijah and his uncle Abu Talib both died.

Allah Yerhamo (fem. *yerhama***):** "May God have mercy of his/her soul", (said when
someone dies)

Youm al Qiyama: The Day of Judgment. Day of Standing, of Resurrection

Youm El-Deen: Judgment Day

Youm: A unit of time usually used for a day but with no set length; day or era

Youm: Day (of)...

Youmul Qiyamah: The Day of (standing for) Judgment.

Zabiha (Zabihah): Islamic method of slaughtering an animal. Meat that has been slaughtered in accordance with Islamic requirements. Slaughter in accordance with Islam.

Zabur (Za boor): The Arabic name for the Psalms of David.

Zahid: Ascetic

Zahir: Exterior meaning. Manifest aspects of God as distinct from the hidden or batin, hence literal or exoteric meaning of Qur'an or hadith; outward, apparent God as the Manifest contrasted with batin

Zahiri: 'Outer' reality of Islamic rites and rituals. 'External' meaning of the divine revelation. Exoteric dimensions of Islam.

Zaidi: A branch of the Shi'a usually designated as moderate that is the closest to the Sunnis in doctrine and law. Zaidism has for long been the dominant form of Islam in Yemen. Islamic sub sect of Shia. *Shia Muslim sect* Zaidis share the first four Imams of Twelver Shia—Ali, Hussein, Hassan, and Zain al Abidin, a grandson of Imam Ali, a son-in-law of the Prophet Muhammad (AD 570-632)—but follow a different line with Zaid, son of Muhammad ibn al Hanafiya and half-brother of Imam Hussein ibn Ali. The Zaidi state of Yemen, established by Imam Yahya ibn Hussein al Rassi in (North) Yemen in AD 898 continued, with some interruptions, until 1962.

Zakah: (Purifying Alms) Literally means purification, whence it is used to express a portion of property bestowed in alms, as a means of purifying the person concerned and the remainder of his property. It is among the five pillars of Islam and refers to the mandatory amount that a Muslim must pay out of his property. The detailed rules of **zakah** have been laid down in books of **Fiqh**. (A) true charity. (Purifying Alms) literally means purification, whence it is used to express a portion of property bestowed in alms, as a means of purifying the person concerned and the remainder of his property.

Zakat: (third pillar of Islam): Annual alms tax or tithe of 2.5 per cent levied on wealth and distributed to the poor. *(Arabic: derivative of zakaa, to be pure)*: The performing of *zakat*, mentioned in the Qur'an as the "freewill offering for 'poor and needy...the ransoming of slaves, debtors in God's way and the traveler", was later refined as obligatory charity by the believer and included in the five pillars of Islam. *Zakat* was prescribed as a religious tax and regulated. The tax varying from 10 percent on crops to 2.5 percent on merchandise and gold and silver. An annual tax on property paid by Muslim for charity purposes or to pay for government expenses. Charity. Annual alms tax or tithe of 2.5 per cent levied on wealth and distributed to the poor.

Zalim: The wrong-doer, he who exceeds the limits of right, the unjust.

Zalimun: Polytheists, wrong doers and unjust.

ZamZam: A sacred spring in Mecca that dates back to the time of Abraham; well that sprang to save Hagar and Ishmael in Arabia. A sacred water well near Mecca from which all pilgrims drink and with which a dead person was washed before burial.

Zandaqa: heresy

Zanna: (Arabic) guesswork. Term used in the Koran for pointless theological speculation. The Christian doctrines of incarnation and trinity; blasphemous in Islam.

Zaouia: Building containing a marabout, a sacred figure or a mystical Sufi brotherhood.

Zar: Exorcism ceremonies.

Zarqa: Zarqa or Zerka, in the Bible, river, 80 mi (129 km) long, rising in the hills W of Amman, N Jordan, and flowing generally north, then west, to the Jordan River; it is the ancient Jabbok. On its southern bank Jacob wrestled with the angel

Zawiya: (Arabic "Corner, Angle") Used variously by the medieval sources for khanqahs hospices or even small madrasas. These divergences all presupport however an abode for teaching shaykh around whom pupils congregated. Ziwiyas were often endowed but unlike madrasas neither endowment nor a strict constitution were necessary prerequisites of their existence. Corner, building for Sufi activities. Literally corner, a sufi center. Residence or place of teaching of a Sufi **sheikh;** similar to a monastery. A Sufi lodge.

Zayd ibn Thabit: (Scribe)

Zaydi: Supporters of the revolt of Zayd ibn Ali who were prepared to support any descendent of Ali and Fatima who rose up as Imam against the illegitimate rulers of Sunni Islam; moral offenses invalidated the imamate and a candidate of greater virtue then had in the Area south of the Caspian and in the Yemen in the 8th and 9th centuries and persisted in the latter.

Zikr: Voluntary daily meditation or Divine Remembrance by Sufis, requiring the repetition of verses from the Quran or God's Beautiful Names. Often practiced to cure mental or physical illness. Remembrance of Allah as an act of worship, invocation. For Sufis, **zikr** is a spiritual exercise involving the invocation of Allah's divine names or a sacred formula under the direction of a spiritual master.

Zillij: Slippery tiles, used in decorating mosques.

Zina: Means illegal sexual intercourse and embraces both fornication and adultery. Fornication as judged by the Shari'a. Illegal sexual intercourse, including fornication, adultery, rape, and prostitution. Sexual relations outside marriage, including both adultery and fortification prohibited in the Quran.

Zindiq: Heresy. In so far it had a specialized sense; it applied to dualist Manichaen heresies which were prevalent in eastern Islam in the 9th and 10th century. However as extirpators of zindiq in their inscriptions are not precise and appear to have regarded any opposition to themselves as heresy.

Zindiqs: Non-Muslims concealing their unbelief, falsely pretending that they are members of the ummah; mostly Zoroastrians and Manicheans.

Ziyy Islami: Islamic dress

Zuharah: A Meccan clan.

Zuhd: Asceticism

Zuhr: One of the five obligatory prayers which is performed after the sun has passed the meridian; noon prayer; the afternoon prayer.

Zuhrah: A clan

Zulfiqar: Sword of Ali presented to him by Muhammad.

Zulm: Literally means placing a thing where it does not belong. Technically, it refers to exceeding the right and hence committing wrong or injustice.

END***END

History of the Jews and Israel

Saul Silas Fathi

(ISBN 978-0-9777117-3-4)

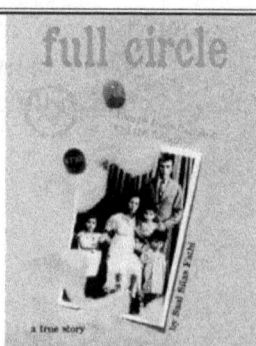

full circle

a true story

by Saul Silas Fathi

(ISBN 978-0-9777117-8-9)

About the Author

Saul Silas Fathi was born to a prominent Jewish family in Baghdad, Iraq. At age 10, he and his younger brother were smuggled out of Baghdad through Iran and eventually reached the newly formed state of Israel. He began writing a diary at age 11 and had several stories published in Israeli youth magazines.

Saul enrolled at the Israel Airforce Academy of Aeronautics, a 4-year program, where he earned his high-school diploma and became certified in electrical engineering. In 1958, he worked his way to Brazil where he nearly starved. Through perseverance and luck, he started his own electrical business and earned a patent for climate-controlled windows used in the building of Brasilia, Brazil.

In 1960, he came to the U.S. on a student exchange visa, studying sculpture at the Brooklyn Museum of Art and American history and public speaking at the New School of Social Studies. After 8 months, Saul volunteered to serve in the U.S. Army for three years, having been promised a college education and U.S. citizenship at the conclusion of his duties. After Basic Training in Fort Benning, Georgia, he was sent to helicopter school at Fort Bragg, North Carolina, and there enrolled at the University Of Virginia. Within a few months, Saul was shipped to South Korea where he served as Chief Electrical Technician with the 1st Cavalry Division, 15th Aviation Company, the famed helicopter division in the Vietnam War.

Back in the U.S., Saul battled the immigration department while studying at the University of Virginia, finally earning a Bachelor of Science degree in electrical engineering. This launched an impressive career as a high-level executive with several Fortune-500 companies. Later, he founded and managed three high-tech companies.

Saul retired in 2003 and began writing his memoirs, Full Circle: Escape from Baghdad and the Return. Today, he lives in Long Island, New York, with his wife Rachelle. They have three U.S.-born daughters and two grandchildren. He is also a certified linguist, fluent in English, Hebrew, Arabic, and Portuguese.

COMPELLING LECTURES!!!

SUBJECTS (Average 2 Hours):

1. The War in Iraq: A Unique Perspective
2. Prospects for War with Iran: Options
3. History of Islam and the Middle-East
4. Jewish Life in Arab Countries
5. Current (International) Affairs
6. Cosmology: The Big Bang, Black Holes and UFO's
7. Saladin and the Crusades
8. Full Circle: Escape from Baghdad and the return
9. Biblical Stories: From Abraham to Jesus
10. Great Women in World History

27 Broadlawn Drive Central Islip, NY 11722-4616
Tel/Fax: (631) 232-1638 • www.saulsilasfathi.com • fathi@optonline.net

DETAILS ON NEXT PAGE ✦

***

Saul Silas Fathi

Glossary of Arabic Terms

www.ingramcontent.com/pod-product-compliance
Lightning Source LLC
Chambersburg PA
CBHW061600110426
42742CB00038B/1855